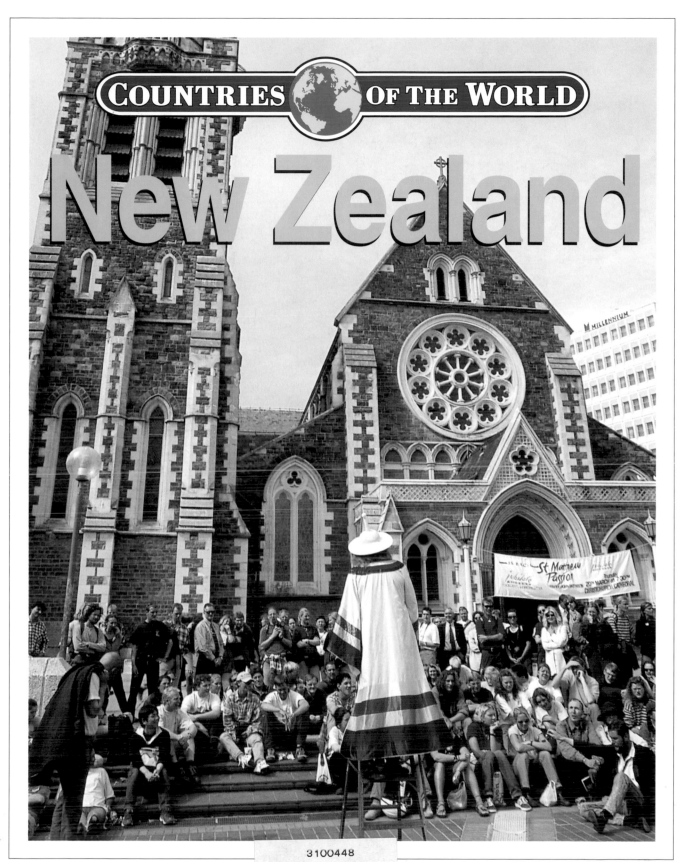

COUNTRIES OF THE WORLD

New Zealand

Gareth Stevens Publishing
A WORLD ALMANAC EDUCATION GROUP COMPANY

About the Author: Ayesha Ercelawn lives and works in the United States. She has extensive experience as a freelance writer and has written and edited many children's books.

Acknowledgments: The publishers would like to thank Helen Ough Dealy for her assistance with the book.

PICTURE CREDITS
ANA Press Agency: 19
Archive Photos: 31 (top), 48, 55, 74, 78, 79, 80, 81, 82, 84
BES Stock: 59 (bottom)
Susanna Burton: 20, 25, 47, 87
Camera Press: 29 (right), 54
Helen Ough Dealy: 90
Focus Team – Italy: 40
Lee Foster: 9 (bottom)
Haga Library, Japan: 38
HBL Network Photo Agency: 34, 36
Dave G. Houser: 18 (top), 33
Hutchison Library: 1, 3 (bottom), 26, 43, 52, 57, 67
The Illustrated London News: 49
Earl Kowall: 73
Nazima Kowall: 3 (top), 12, 28 (top)
Life File Photo Library: 8
North Wind Picture Archives: 10, 11 (bottom)
NZTB: 64, 83, 91
Christine Osborne Pictures: 7, 18 (bottom), 41
David Simson: 3 (center), 21, 23, 37
Topham Picturepoint: cover, 4, 5, 11 (top), 13, 14, 15 (bottom), 16, 29 (left), 31 (bottom), 44, 45, 51, 56, 58, 60, 65, 66, 76, 85, 89
Travel Ink: 50, 69
Trip Photo Library: 2, 6, 9 (top), 17, 22, 24, 27, 28 (bottom), 30, 32, 35, 39, 42, 46, 53, 59 (top), 61, 62 (both), 63, 68, 70, 71, 72, 75, 77
Vision Photo Agency/Hulton Getty: 15 (top)

Digital Scanning by Superskill Graphics Pte Ltd

Written by
AYESHA ERCELAWN

Edited by
PAUL ROZARIO

Designed by
LYNN CHIN

Picture research by
SUSAN JANE MANUEL

First published in North America in 2001 by
Gareth Stevens Publishing
A World Almanac Education Group Company
330 West Olive Street, Suite 100
Milwaukee, Wisconsin 53212 USA

For a free color catalog describing
Gareth Stevens' list of high-quality books
and multimedia programs, call
1-800-542-2595 (USA) or
1-800-461-9120 (CANADA).
Gareth Stevens Publishing's
Fax: (414) 332-3567.

© **TIMES MEDIA PRIVATE LIMITED 2001**
Originated and designed by
Times Editions
an imprint of Times Media Private Limited
Times Centre, 1 New Industrial Road
Singapore 536196
http://www.timesone.com.sg/te

Library of Congress Cataloging-in-Publication Data
Ercelawn, Ayesha.
New Zealand / by Ayesha Ercelawn.
p. cm. -- (Countries of the world)
Includes bibliographical references and index.
ISBN 0-8368-2332-X (lib. bdg.)
1. New Zealand--Juvenile literature. [1. New Zealand.] I. Title.
II. Countries of the World (Milwaukee, Wis.)
DU408.E74   2001
993--dc21   00-057399

Printed in Malaysia

1 2 3 4 5 6 7 8 9 05 04 03 02 01

Contents

AN OVERVIEW OF NEW ZEALAND

The land that the Maori called *Aotearoa* (ah-oh-tay-ah-RROH-ah), or "land of the long white cloud," is better known to the rest of the world as New Zealand. This cluster of islands lies in the South Pacific Ocean and is isolated geographically, if not culturally, from much of the rest of the world. New Zealand is part of a large island group known as Polynesia. The Maori, a Polynesian people, were its earliest inhabitants. Europeans, the British primarily, colonized the country in the nineteenth century. Since that time, New Zealand has been a multicultural society that includes Samoans, Tongans, and Asians. Calling themselves "Kiwis" after their national bird, New Zealanders pride themselves on working toward a society that treats all its citizens equally.

Opposite: **The people of New Zealand live in idyllic surroundings. Lake Wakatipu, on the South Island, is a good example.**

Below: **New Zealand's spectacular ski resorts at Whakapapa, North Island, attract visitors from around the world.**

THE FLAG OF NEW ZEALAND

New Zealand used the British Union Jack as its flag in the nineteenth century, when it was still a British colony. By the early twentieth century, however, a strong feeling of patriotism had developed in the country, and the current flag was then adopted. It is based on the Blue Ensign, the flag used by New Zealand ships. The Union Jack appears in the upper left corner. The Southern Cross, a constellation visible in the Southern Hemisphere, appears on the right as four red stars on a blue background. New Zealanders fly the flag on Waitangi Day, ANZAC Day, and on the British monarch's birthday.

Geography

Spectacular Landscape

New Zealand is an island country in the South Pacific Ocean. Its nearest large neighbor, Australia, lies more than 1,000 miles (1,609 kilometers) to the northwest. Little mystery is involved in the English names of New Zealand's two main islands: North Island and South Island. Several dozen smaller islands are also part of New Zealand's territory, including Stewart Island and the Chatham Islands. Most New Zealanders live on the North Island. Wellington, the capital city, is on the North Island, as is the largest city and port, Auckland.

New Zealand's spectacular landscape is formed as a result of two continental plates colliding with each other — the Pacific plate and the Australian-Indian plate. The mountainous terrain of the North Island was created by intense volcanic activity, some of which continues to this day. The largest natural lake in New Zealand, Lake Taupo, is actually an ancient volcanic crater. It is

Below: **Lake Taupo, North Island, was formed centuries ago by a volcanic eruption and is the source of the Waikato, New Zealand's longest river.**

bordered to the south by a volcanic plateau, which includes the magnificent Tongariro, Ruapehu, and Ngauruhoe volcanoes. Ngauruhoe and Ruapehu continue to be active; Ruapehu volcano last erupted in 1998.

Glaciers and Fiords

Much more rugged landscape characterizes the South Island. The Southern Alps, extending north to south, include New Zealand's highest peak, Mount Cook, at 12,349 feet (3,764 meters). Spectacular glaciers, including the Fox and Franz Josef glaciers, descend from the mountains and move toward the western coast. Glacier water and melting snows feed the South Island's many lakes. The Canterbury Plains to the east have been formed over time from mountain sediment carried down by rivers. To the southeast, central Otago is an area of gentle scenery, with rolling hills and plains. Farther south and west, long inlets of the sea called fiords cut into the land, creating a jagged coastline. This area is known as Fiordland, and much of it is protected under Fiordland National Park.

Above: **Mount Cook, on the South Island, is the highest peak in New Zealand. It is aptly named Aoraki, or "the cloud piercer," in the Maori language.**

HISSING GEYSERS AND SMOKING CRATERS

Waters from natural hot springs in the town of Rotorua and its surrounding areas on the North Island are believed to be therapeutic. The waters, with their high mineral content, are said to help those with arthritis, eczema, and nervous diseases.

(A Closer Look, page 50)

SAVING LAKE MANAPOURI

A thirteen-year campaign to save Lake Manapouri was a milestone for the conservation movement in New Zealand.
(A Closer Look, page 64)

Climate

Surrounded by ocean waters, New Zealand has a mild, moist climate. Because the country is south of the equator, the coldest month of winter is July, and the warmest summer months are January and February. Rain falls throughout most of the year, with generally much more rain falling in winter than in summer.

The country's mountain ranges also have a strong influence on climate patterns. Running north to south, these ranges form a barrier against winds carrying moisture from the west. As a result, most of the rain falls on western slopes, while eastern areas are much drier. For example, Milford Sound, on the western coast of the South Island, receives up to 300 inches (760 centimeters) of rainfall a year, while east of the Southern Alps, regions may get less than 20 inches (50 cm) a year.

Other regional variations in climate also exist. For example, the northern tip of the North Island is warm and humid all year, while the central plateau has greater temperature fluctuations, with hot weather in summer and frosts or snow in winter.

THE MOA: HUNTED TO EXTINCTION

The moa was a large flightless bird that could reach a height of 13 feet (4 m). Before humans arrived, the giant moa roamed the plains and forested regions of the entire country. The early Maori used them as their main source of meat but had hunted them to extinction by the early 1800s.

Plant and Animal Life

Because New Zealand is isolated from other continents, many of its plants and animals are unique to its islands — about 90 percent of New Zealand's plant life is found nowhere else on Earth. Most trees here are evergreens, or trees that keep their leaves all year round. Many of the original forests of giant kauri trees in the extreme north have been cut down, although a few scattered patches remain in parks and nature reserves. Other areas are covered by rain forests, with lush ferns and diverse wildlife.

New Zealand has many native birds, including various flightless species, such as the well-known kiwi; the kakapo, the world's largest flightless parrot; the takahe; and the weka. Few land animals existed on New Zealand's islands before the arrival of European settlers, and the only mammals up to that time were two species of bats. The flightless birds, therefore, had no natural defenses against any land predators. Settlers brought rats, deer, and rabbits from Europe and wallabies and brush-tailed possums from Australia. Along with pets such as cats and dogs, these animals have since become a major threat to the survival of the native species of flightless birds.

The neighboring waters of the South Pacific Ocean and Tasman Sea support many ocean creatures, from tuna and cod to Hector's dolphins, sperm whales, humpback whales, and orcas.

Above: **The kaka beak (*Clianthus puniceus*) is a plant species native to New Zealand. It was once common in the wild. Today, however, most specimens grow in gardens.**

RATS

Rats are the number one pests brought in by European settlers, but Europeans were not the only ones to bring predators to New Zealand. The Maori introduced the Pacific rat, or kiore, which has caused significant damage to native bird and insect species.

Left: **Named for its call, "ki-wi," the kiwi is a native flightless bird and the national symbol of New Zealand. Four species exist in the country, but all are now threatened due to predators and loss of habitat.**

History

Maori Tribes

New Zealand was "new" indeed to the first Europeans to discover it in the seventeenth century. The land, however, had been settled since at least the ninth century by the Maori. These people had arrived by canoe from Polynesia, a group of islands east of New Zealand in the South Pacific Ocean. The Maori introduced and cultivated some of their own vegetables, such as taro, but the moa, a large flightless bird, was their main staple. Gradually, however, the moa was hunted to extinction. By the nineteenth century, the Maori were mainly farmers, with the majority settled in villages in the warmer, northern parts of the country. Each Maori tribe had its own chief, and land was communally owned.

Below: **Early Europeans went to New Zealand in the eighteenth century to hunt whales for their valuable oil. The early twentieth century saw shore-based whaling stations in operation until the 1930s and 1940s.**

The Arrival of Europeans

A Dutch sailor, Abel Tasman, was the first European to sight New Zealand. In 1642, he arrived off the coast of West Coast on the South Island. His only attempt to land resulted in a conflict with the local Maori tribe, and several of his men were killed. Tasman himself never set foot in New Zealand.

The Dutch were not quick to return but left behind their legacy by naming the country "Nieuw Zeeland," after a province in the Netherlands. The next European to show interest in New Zealand was the British explorer Captain James Cook. He landed on the North Island in 1769, established friendly relations with the Maori, and began to systematically explore the two main islands by sea. Captain Cook's favorable reports encouraged other Europeans to travel and settle in New Zealand, particularly those in search of sealskins, whale oil, New Zealand flax, and timber.

New Zealand (along with Australia) became an important base for whalers, sealers, and traders. Russell (then known as Kororareka), the first European settlement, was a major stopover for Australian, American, British, and French whalers and sealers.

Other Europeans were attracted by the mild climate and fertile farming lands. The Maori were involved in all this new activity as well, trading with the Europeans to obtain muskets, weapons new to them; rum; and other goods.

Above: The Maori drove off the Dutch, the first Europeans who attempted to land in New Zealand.

Below: Captain James Cook, a British navigator, sailed to New Zealand on his ship, the *Endeavour.* He not only charted New Zealand's two major islands but later also mapped much of Australia's coastline.

Above: **The introduction of the railway in New Zealand helped the country's economic growth in the late nineteenth century. This early steam engine now serves as a tourist attraction on the North Island.**

Maori Society

The use of muskets spread among the Maori with devastating consequences. Chief Hongi Hika was the first to seize upon the weapon's potential and waged war on many of his rival tribes. Tribal wars spread throughout the islands, displacing the Maori population. European traders and missionaries started to found colonies in areas unsettled by the warfare. By the 1830s, the Maori realized that they were destroying their own race, and intertribal wars gradually ended. Meanwhile, many Maori also died after contracting new diseases that came with the European settlers. The Maori's social structure disintegrated further as missionaries introduced Christianity and Western agricultural methods.

A British Colony

As the 1840s began, the British decided they needed to establish some form of control over the new colonies and sent William Hobson as lieutenant governor. On February 6, 1840, Hobson, along with representatives of the British Crown and a number of Maori chiefs, signed the Treaty of Waitangi, under which New Zealand became a British colony. According to the treaty, the British government was to protect the rights of the Maori, and Maori lands could be bought only by the British Crown.

TREATY OF WAITANGI

Celebrations are held each year on February 6 to commemorate the signing of the Treaty of Waitangi in 1840.
(A Closer Look, page 72)

Land Wars

Demand for land by Europeans grew, however, as more and more colonists arrived. Soon, the Treaty of Waitangi was being ignored. Fighting over land broke out on the North Island and continued off and on until the 1870s. In 1846, British troops defeated in battle a principal Maori leader, Hone Heke. Peace then reigned until 1860, when fighting resumed. The Maori lost most of their land to the colonists in the land wars of the 1860s and 1870s.

Meanwhile, strong anti-European feelings began developing in the 1850s, as some tribes in the central part of the country decided not to sell any more land to the settlers. They appointed one of their chiefs, Potatau Te Wherowhero, king in 1858.

Left: Wars between Maori tribes continued until the 1830s, when they realized that intertribal fighting was destroying their race. This nineteenth-century print by a European artist shows a Maori warrior dressed in traditional military attire.

13

Colonial History

By the 1840s, European settlers, then ruled by the British Crown, were demanding representational government. Governor George Grey helped draft the New Zealand Constitution Act of 1852, which granted New Zealand self-government.

New Zealand's economy grew rapidly in the late nineteenth century. Much of the hilly land of the South Island was ideal for sheep-grazing, and soon farmers were exporting wool to Australia and Britain. In the 1860s, gold was discovered in Otago, South Island. For a fleeting period, people from Australia and California, in particular, rushed over to search for gold.

Dairy farms, orchards, and vegetable farms were established on the North Island. The introduction of refrigerated ships in 1882 dramatically boosted the economy as farmers began to export meat and dairy products to Britain and Europe.

Two major political parties emerged in the late nineteenth and early twentieth centuries — the Liberal Party and the Labour Party. Both parties put forward progressive social policies. By this time, nationalist sentiments had also grown strong, and New Zealanders were starting to consider their land a separate nation. They were granted more autonomy from Britain in 1907, when the country became a dominion territory. New Zealand's involvement in World Wars I and II boosted national pride. In both wars, New Zealanders fought on the side of Britain. In 1947, New Zealand finally became fully independent from Britain.

THREE CITIES, THREE HISTORIES

Signs of New Zealand's colonial settlement history are still evident in different towns. The distinctly rolled "r" in the speech of Dunedin's residents gives away the Scottish heritage of the city. Christchurch, on the other hand, was settled by the English, while Akaroa was the first French settlement.
(A Closer Look, page 68)

Left: The discovery of gold in the Otago region, South Island, in the 1860s attracted hordes of prospectors from nearby Australia and faraway California.

Abel Tasman (1603–1659)

Dutch navigator Abel Tasman, the first European to sight New Zealand, arrived off the coast of the West Coast region, South Island, in 1642. He was on a mission to discover riches for the Dutch East India Company and to find a southern shipping route to South America. He saw what he described as a "great land uplifted high" (the Southern Alps). Four of his men were killed when his attempt to make contact with the inhabitants was rebuffed by an attack. Tasman sailed away, and New Zealand was left alone for 127 years, until Captain Cook's expedition in 1769.

Abel Tasman

Sir George Grey (1812–1898)

Sir George Grey, a British colonial administrator, played a long and influential role in New Zealand politics. He was governor during the land wars from 1845 to 1853 and again from 1861 to 1868. Accused of being autocratic, he nevertheless had great respect for the Maori people and their customs, learning their language and establishing friendly relations with them. Grey became a scholar of Maori culture and wrote about their mythology and oral history. He brought peace to New Zealand's new colonies during his first term by making agreements with some Maori groups while successfully defeating other chiefs, such as Hone Heke and Kawati. The New Zealand Constitution Act, which gave the settlers self-governance, was also created during Grey's time in office. He later served twenty years in the country's parliament (1874–1894) and was premier from 1877 to 1879.

Sir George Grey

Potatau Te Wherowhero (1800–1860)

Potatau Te Wherowhero (King Potatau I), a chief of the Waikato, was declared Maori king in 1858. Son of a famous fighting chief, he himself became a famous leader through his battle campaigns against the Ngati Toa and Ngati Awa tribes. His prestige among the Maori made him a key figure. Some of his Maori followers decided not to sell any more land to the European settlers. Potatau, however, established friendly relations with the British governor, George Grey. His successors continue to work toward securing Maori rights.

Government and the Economy

A Parliamentary Democracy

New Zealand has a parliamentary form of government, and the British monarch, Queen Elizabeth II, is the formal head of state. A governor-general appointed by the Queen represents her in New Zealand, but he has little power in reality.

New Zealand's parliament, or House of Representatives, consists of 120 members who are elected to three-year terms. All citizens eighteen years and older can vote. The leader of the party that wins the most seats in a parliamentary election becomes prime minister. The prime minister and the ministers responsible for the different areas of government together form the cabinet, the executive arm of the government. Two parties dominate the country's politics, the National Party and the Labour Party. Other, smaller parties exist, but they rarely win elections.

Below: **The "Beehive" in Wellington houses the cabinet ministers. Designed by a British architect, Sir Basil Spence, it was completed in 1980.**

The prime minister appoints members to the cabinet, which runs various government departments, such as the Department of Conservation, the Department of Labour, and the Department of Justice. New bills are proposed by the prime minister and the cabinet; a majority in the parliament must then pass the bill before it can become law.

The Constitution is a collection of statutes and customary laws. Some of the laws are derived from British laws; others were more recently enacted by the New Zealand parliament. The Constitution Act of 1852 created the parliament, while the recent Constitution Act of 1986 consolidated laws created since 1852. The Privy Council in Britain is the highest court, followed by the Court of Appeal in New Zealand. The latter court hears cases that have been appealed from lower courts. District courts hear civic and criminal cases. Juries are part of the judicial system, and twelve jurors are selected for each trial.

Local government is divided into four categories: territorial authorities, regional authorities, district councils, and special purpose authorities, including a wallaby board, which works toward controlling the population of wallabies.

Above: **Mounted police help keep the peace on a Christchurch street. New Zealand inherited some of its laws from the British system.**

FROM TEA TO VOTES

Helen Clark, the current prime minister, comes from a strong tradition of women's involvement in New Zealand politics. New Zealand was the first country to give women the right to vote. Much of this achievement was brought about by the efforts of Kate Sheppard, a suffragette who lived in the nineteenth century.
(A Closer Look, page 48)

Farming

New Zealand's mild climate and frequent rainfall have made it well suited to farming and raising livestock. Sheep are raised throughout the country for their wool and meat, both lamb and mutton. Along with dairy products and beef, sheep products are among New Zealand's most important exports. Large sheep and cattle farms are called "stations." Many of the dairy farms are on the North Island.

New Zealand is one of the few places where deer are raised on farms. They were introduced into the country in the nineteenth century for hunting, but they soon became a nuisance. Deer are now raised on small farms surrounded by high fences so they cannot escape and destroy native vegetation. All parts of the animal are valuable. Deer meat, or venison, and hides are exported to Europe, and antler velvet is exported to Asia, where it is used in medicine.

Fruits such as kiwifruit, tamarillos, and passionfruit are grown for export and have become popular worldwide. Other crops, including wheat, barley, and maize, are grown for the local market. Great Britain was once New Zealand's most important trading partner. Now, the United States, Japan, Australia, and Middle East countries have become substantial trading partners.

KIWIFRUIT
The luscious kiwifruit is almost always associated with New Zealand. It is not, however, originally from New Zealand.
(*A Closer Look*, page 56)

Below: Deer are raised on small farms. Deer meat is exported to Europe, while antler velvet goes to Asia to be used in medicines.

Industry and Resources

Forestry has become an increasingly important industry in recent years. Most New Zealand timber now comes from pine plantations, rather than from native forests, and some land unsuitable for farming has been planted with pine trees originally from California. New Zealand's stunning scenery — including forests, mountains, glaciers, and coastlines — has made tourism an important part of the economy.

New Zealand's relative isolation from other countries has led to the development of a broad manufacturing industry. Among the manufactured products are textiles, leather goods, plastics, building supplies, and agricultural machinery. Two steel companies and other industries produce highly specialized agricultural, medical, and veterinary equipment. A small, but growing, aircraft-building industry also exists.

The country has very few mineral resources apart from some coal and natural gas. Most minerals, therefore, have to be imported. Gold is still mined in central North Island, on the Coromandel Peninsula, and, to a smaller extent, in West Coast.

Above: **Tourists are taken on a harbor cruise off Auckland. New Zealand's spectacular scenery attracts more than 1.4 million overseas visitors a year.**

People and Lifestyle

A Strong European Culture

New Zealanders have nicknamed themselves "Kiwis," after their national bird, the kiwi. The country is relatively sparsely settled, with a population of about 3.8 million. The majority of its people — about 75 percent — are of European descent, mainly from England, Scotland, and Ireland. Others have ancestors from Italy, the Balkans, the Netherlands, Germany, Greece, or Scandinavia. Because of this history of settlement, New Zealand's culture is strongly European.

Maori are the largest minority, making up about 10 percent of the population. The word *maori* means "normal" in the Maori language. It was adopted by the Maori to distinguish themselves from the first European settlers, whom the Maori called *pakeha*. The term *pakeha* is still commonly used throughout the country. As Maori increasingly moved to the cities, their culture was swamped with European influences, and the people lost touch with their language and traditions.

Left: **This family sits down to an evening meal, often the only time when families get together.**

Above: **This mural depicts an exchange of greetings between a Maori in traditional dress and an immigrant from Vietnam. The children of New Zealand's different ethnic communities play together in the background.**

Maori culture, however, is now making a comeback and is playing an increasingly larger role in New Zealand society. More and more young Maori are learning the Maori language and reconnecting with their tribal history. Some pakeha are also embracing elements of Maori culture.

Asians and immigrants from other Pacific Islands make up the rest of the population. Samoans and Tongans, for instance, have introduced their cultures to New Zealand. Samoan rugby is now popular, and Polynesian foods, such as taro and yams, are becoming increasingly available. Immigration from Asian countries has been high in recent years, and the country has sizable communities of Indians, Chinese, and Vietnamese.

Migration to the Cities

Most New Zealanders have moved out of rural areas and into towns and cities to find jobs. Only a small fraction of people, such as those working on sheep stations, live in the countryside. The North Island is more heavily populated than the South Island, and New Zealand's most populous cities, Auckland and Wellington, are located there. The largest city on the South Island is Christchurch.

Left: **The marae, the open space in front of traditional meeting houses, is where important events, such as weddings and funerals, are held. This marae is in the Bay of Plenty region.**

Maori Community Life

Maori community life centers around the traditional tribal meeting house and the large open space, or *marae* (mah-rah-EE), in front of the meeting house. This is a sacred space where many important life events, such as weddings, funerals, and twenty-first birthday celebrations, are held.

Strict rules surround a marae and the meeting house, and people must follow certain customs when visiting. For instance, no one may speak or walk around till the Maori elders have performed the formal welcoming ceremony, which includes addressing the ancestral spirits, giving welcome speeches, singing songs, and performing a formal dance. When the welcome is over, people greet one another in the traditional Maori custom by pressing noses together.

Maori retain membership in their tribe even if members are scattered throughout the country. On special occasions, some Maori who live in urban areas return to their ancestral, rural marae. Others attend the new marae that have been built more recently in cities. Many younger, urban Maori are going back to their traditional roots and asking for more say in tribal affairs.

A Land for All?

Equal rights matter to all New Zealanders. Many of the early European settlers were working- or middle-class immigrants who wanted to get away from the rigid class structures in Europe. They worked toward creating a community with social equality.

Today, the government tries to provide equal opportunities and care for everyone. Education is free up to the secondary level. New Zealanders also receive financial and health benefits from the government. Public hospital and emergency care services, for instance, are funded by the government. Single parents also receive help to support their children.

The practice of equal rights, however, has not always been easy. Although intermarriages between Maori and pakeha have become more common, racial tensions exist. Maori, as well as the other minorities, struggle against discrimination and tend to have higher rates of unemployment. Maori also suffer from more health problems and have much shorter life spans, on average, than non-Maori New Zealanders. Many Maori are campaigning for the return of their traditional lands, with the more radical among them calling for a separate Maori government.

Below: New Zealand is an increasingly diverse society, including the Maori, Asians, Pacific islanders, and descendants of Europeans. Despite some problems, relations among ethnic communities are generally good, and New Zealand is proud of its record of racial harmony.

Education

Since its early years as a colony, a great emphasis has been placed on education in New Zealand. Education is free up to the age of fifteen, and schooling is compulsory for New Zealanders between the ages of six and fifteen. Some children begin preschool when they are three years old. Religious groups, such as the Roman Catholic Church, run some primary and secondary schools. Although private, these schools receive funding from the government and must maintain certain standards of teaching. Maori children can attend special school groups called *te kohanga reo* (teh koh-HAH-nyah RREH-oh), or language nests, where children are immersed in Maori language and cultural sessions in an effort to preserve their cultural identity.

Secondary education usually begins at the age of thirteen, when students enter what is known as Form 3. In their last year of school, or Form 5, students take the School Certificate exam. After further exams and schooling, they can go on to college.

Left: **Maori boys listen attentively in the assembly hall of Te Aute Boys' College in the Hawke's Bay region, North Island.**

Children who live in remote rural areas, such as sheep stations, that are far from bus routes, do not get to skip school. They receive their education over the radio and through the mail. The New Zealand Correspondence School in Wellington is a government-run school that broadcasts lessons daily. Students also receive lessons in the mail, then send their homework back to the teachers, who try to visit their pupils once or twice a year.

Above: **Reading in front of her classmates helps this girl gain confidence in her own reading skills. New Zealand has a very high literacy rate.**

Universities

New Zealand has eight major universities. Over 100,000 students attend these universities, which are state funded but run by independent councils. The country also has about twenty-five publicly owned polytechnics, which are attended by another 100,000 students. These polytechnics teach a variety of applied sciences and technical courses. Some polytechnics also award degrees. Five colleges of education offer courses in teacher training, and the National Council of Adult Education offers an extensive program in further education for adults.

Religion

New Zealand does not have an official religion. Just over three-fifths of the population, however, are Christians belonging to the Anglican, Presbyterian, Roman Catholic, and Methodist denominations. Small minorities of other religions also exist, including Hindus and Jews. Most Maori were converted to Christianity by missionaries in the nineteenth century. Religion, however, does not play a large role in most people's lives. New Zealanders rarely go to church, and a large number of them claim no religious affiliation.

During the land wars with European settlers in the 1860s, Maori cults sprang up. Pai Marire, or Hauhauism, a mix of Jewish, Christian, and native beliefs, was the first of many Maori religious movements that swept across the North Island. The term *hauhau* came from the warriors' battle cry.

Later in the nineteenth century, the Ringatu Church was founded by Te Kooti Rikirangi, a guerrilla leader. The Ringatu Church still has many thousands of followers, with its greatest influence being in the Bay of Plenty region of the North Island. Followers of the Ringatu Church have a regular ritual of chanting and hymns on the eleventh evening of every month. Other Maori belong to the Ratana Church. People of this faith call themselves Nga Morehu, or "the remnants."

Traditional Maori Beliefs

Before European settlement, Maori society revolved around the *iwi* (ee-WEE), or tribe, or around the *hapu* (HAH-poo), or subtribe. Maori religious beliefs included many different gods, representing the sky, the sea, mountains, war, or other aspects of life. The idea of a life force or spirit in all things was central to Maori beliefs. Traditional legends, including the story of creation, revolved around these gods. The land of New Zealand, for instance, was said to be formed when the god Maui went fishing in a canoe. His hook caught a giant fish, which became the North Island. His canoe became the South Island, and Stewart Island was formed from his anchor.

Maori ceremonies were traditionally held in the marae, an open space in front of the communal meeting house and home to a tribe's ancestral spirit. Priests communicated directly with the gods. Many Maori ceremonies are still held in the marae.

Above: **A Maori preacher delivers a sermon from the pulpit of St. Paul's Church in the suburb of Putiki, Auckland, on the North Island.**

Opposite: **Christchurch Cathedral is one of New Zealand's best-known churches.**

MIRACLE CURES

Many Maori belong to the Ratana Church. This church was founded by Tahupotiki Wiremu Ratana, a Maori farmer. Known to most people as Bill Ratana, he began having visions in 1919, soon after the end of World War I. Word of his visions and miraculous cures of the sick spread among the Maori, and gradually a new religion was established at Ratana, a town near Wanganui on the North Island. The beliefs of the Ratana Church are basically Christian, with an emphasis on healing through prayer and faith.

Language and Literature

English and Maori are the two official languages of New Zealand. Maori was the only language spoken until the country was settled by the Europeans. English is now the primary language, but Maori is increasingly being used. A Polynesian dialect, Maori shares roots with languages spoken on many other Polynesian islands across the Pacific Ocean.

After New Zealand was settled by the Europeans, the Maori language was spoken less and less, as English became required at school. In the 1960s, however, there was a revival of interest by the Maori in their own culture and language. Now, the Maori language is being taught not only at schools but also at universities. The language was given a further boost in 1987, when the government set up the Maori Language Commission. This organization promotes the use of Maori as a living language and as an ordinary means of communication. The language has become even more widely known with the advent of the Internet, as Maori-English dictionaries and texts of Maori poems, chants, songs, and stories are placed online.

Many place names in New Zealand are Maori words. *Wai* (wah-EE), for example, means "water" and is a common prefix for place names such as Waitangi and Wairakei. Some Maori words have also become part of everyday speech, such as their term *pakeha*, for people of European descent. The Maori greetings *kia ora* (kee-ah OH-rrah), "hello;" *haere mai* (hay-REH mah-EE), "welcome;" and *haere ra* (hay-REH rrah), "farewell," are increasingly used by all people in New Zealand.

Maori Oral Literature

The literary tradition of the Maori is an oral one. Hand gestures, stamping, facial expressions, and music are all important accompaniments to the story. Songs and chants are used to teach history to the next generation. The Maori also perform myths, love poems, war chants, prayers, and laments. In pre-European times, the text was memorized and passed down orally from generation to generation.

Above: **A Maori woman performs a traditional Maori poem at a marae in Whakarewarewa. With the revival of Maori culture, only Maori is spoken inside some tribal meeting houses.**

Above: **The Treaty of Waitangi, signed in 1840, was drafted in both the English and Maori languages.**

New Zealand Literature

New Zealand's first writers in the English language took their inspiration primarily from the traditions of British literature. It was not until the early 1900s that a distinctly New Zealand style of literature began to emerge. Katherine Mansfield (1888–1923) was among the first of these new writers and certainly one of the most influential for following generations. She developed a unique writing style and set many of her short stories in the New Zealand of her childhood.

The first Maori writer to join the English literary scene was Jacqueline Sturm, who was published in 1966 in an anthology of New Zealand short stories. Hone Tuwhare's poems and Witi Ihimaera's short stories clearly established Maori writers among New Zealand's literary community.

Keri Hulme's *The Bone People* won the Booker Prize in 1985 and is probably the most well-known New Zealand book both at home and abroad. Margaret Mahy, a children's writer, is also one of New Zealand's most successful writers. Other popular authors include Dame Ngaio Marsh, Alan Duff, and Philip Temple.

Above: Katherine Mansfield *(left)* is widely known for her short stories. *Prelude*, published in 1918, is a collection of stories that evoke her early childhood in New Zealand. Keri Hulme *(right)* is one of New Zealand's most successful modern-day writers.

Arts

The arts, whether visual, performing, or literary, have been highly encouraged in New Zealand. The government-funded Queen Elizabeth II Arts Council and its successor agency, Creative New Zealand, have provided grants for virtually all artistic and cultural activities, such as theater, music, dance, ballet, and opera. Today, funding for Creative New Zealand comes largely from the profits of government-run lotteries. In 1999, the agency had a budget of NZ $23.7 million. Regional arts councils also provide assistance to local amateur groups and individuals.

Frances Hodgkins (1869–1947) was the first New Zealand painter to gain international recognition. Born in Dunedin on the South Island, she traveled throughout the country, sketching and painting for local newspapers and magazines. She traveled to Britain in 1901 and spent most of the rest of her life in Britain and Europe. Still lifes and landscapes were her primary themes. Today, her work can be seen in many major museums.

ARCHITECTURE

One of the most distinctive cities in New Zealand is Napier, which was rebuilt after it was damaged by an earthquake in 1931. At the time, Art Deco was at the height of its popularity in Europe, so many new buildings in Napier were created in this style. Many of the buildings were designed by Louis Hay, an important New Zealand architect who was inspired by the work of American architect Frank Lloyd Wright.

Left: Auckland is a vibrant city for the arts and home to the Auckland Art Gallery. Here, in the lobby of the gallery, Henry Moore's sculpture entitled "Seated Figure" is on display.

Visual and Performing Arts

New Zealand has a thriving theater, music, and dance scene. The Downstage Theatre in Wellington is well-known for its professional theatrical performances. Dunedin has become the country's music capital and has produced a number of rock bands, including Split ENZ, Straitjacket Fits, the Clean (formerly, the Great Unwashed), and the Chills. Many of these bands have been recorded under the Flying Nun label. Successful New Zealand bands are also popular in Australia.

Cinema is also a growing art form in the country. In recent years, some New Zealand films have become known internationally. Jane Campion, the country's best-known film director, focuses on New Zealand themes. Her film *The Piano*, released in 1993, was set in pioneer days. *An Angel at My Table* (1990) was based on the life of New Zealand writer Janet Frame.

Other New Zealand films, such as *Once Were Warriors* (1995) and *Heavenly Creatures* (1994), have also received international recognition. Lucy Lawless is probably the country's most famous actress. She has become known for her starring role in the television series "Xena, Warrior Princess."

Above: Teen actress Anna Paquin has been acting since the age of nine, when she starred with Holly Hunter in *The Piano*, a role for which she won the 1993 Oscar for Best Supporting Actress. She is one of the youngest actors to have received an Oscar.

Maori Dance

Maori culture has experienced a strong revival in recent years.
An important part of this revival has been achieved through
learning and performing traditional songs and dances. These
long, narrative songs and dances record Maori history.

Dance, like many traditional Maori rituals, is very stylized.
Men dance the *haka* (HAH-kah), war dances once performed
before going into battle. Brandishing clubs or spears, they chant,
grimace, and stick out their tongues threateningly, as they would
at enemies. Women may perform a *poi* (poh-EE), or ball dance,
in which they gracefully twirl balls of fiber while chanting and
swaying. Many tribes have retained ancient poi lyrics, even if
the original movements are no longer the same. At the same
time, new songs, dances, and stories continue to be created today.

Some of the best performers join groups known as *kapa haka*
(KAH-pah HAH-kah) and perform at the Aotearoa Traditional
Performing Arts Festival, a national competition. Some kapa
haka have been performing at the festival since it first started
in 1972, while others are relative newcomers.

Above: **These Maori
men in Waitangi chant
and grimace as they go
through the rituals
of a war dance.**

MAORI PERFORMING ARTS

**Skilled Maori dancers
and singers compete
in regional and national
competitions. Groups
come from around the
country and even from
Australia and the Pacific
Islands to perform at
the Aotearoa Traditional
Performing Arts Festival.**
(*A Closer Look,* page 58).

Carving, Weaving, and Other Arts

Many traditional Maori meeting houses are now used as schools for carving, weaving, and other traditional arts. These arts also play a role in preserving Maori culture. Maori history, for example, is recorded in carvings. Tribal meeting houses, canoes, tools, and jewelry were traditionally carved with elaborate flowing lines and spiral designs. Carved wooden figures called *poupou* (POO-poo) decorate many meeting houses. Patterns represent the wealth of the sea, ancestors, and native plants and animals; the designs usually tell a story. Maori-influenced designs are also seen throughout the country now, whether on airmail envelopes or as the symbol of New Zealand's national airline, Air New Zealand. Basketry, weaving, and a form of wall paneling known as *tukutuku* (too-koo-TOO-koo) are also practiced.

Modern Maori artists such as sculptor Arnold Wilson and painter Ralph Hotere blend traditional styles with new ideas. Te Waka Toi, the Maori arts board of Creative New Zealand, supports Maori artists and recognizes both traditional and modern art forms. Maori art, however, is no longer restricted to the Maori alone; many pakeha have also mastered these crafts.

PRECIOUS POUNAMU

Greenstone, or *pounamu* (poo-NAH-moo), is a prized stone among the Maori and is today used for making earrings and pendants, often in the form of fishhooks.

(A Closer Look, page 62)

Below: This Maori craftsman at the Maori Arts and Crafts Institute in Rotorua carves symbolic patterns into the wooden panel of a traditional house.

Leisure and Festivals

The Great Outdoors

The country's vast areas of wilderness and the diversity of its landscape have made "tramping," or hiking, a very popular activity. Many trails run past scenic and historic sites. They traverse national parks and private land. Hikers can tramp for several days and spend nights camping outdoors in tents.

New Zealand's mountainous terrain tempts both skiers and climbers. Taranaki, Ruapehu, Cook, Tasman, La Perouse, and Sefton are challenging peaks popular with mountain climbers. Other New Zealanders like to swim, sail, scuba dive, surf, or just go fishing.

Team Sports

Team sports, such as rugby, cricket, soccer, and hockey, are favorite sports. Some children, mainly boys, learn to play cricket and rugby as soon as they are able and, by the age of seven, may be happily immersed in cricket or rugby matches.

TRAMPING

New Zealand's natural beauty and diverse wildlife make tramping, or hiking, a rewarding pastime.
(A Closer Look, page 70)

CONQUEROR OF EVEREST

Sir Edmund Hillary is New Zealand's most famous mountain climber. In 1953, Hillary and his Sherpa companion, Tenzing Norgay, became the first climbers to reach the summit of Mount Everest, the world's highest mountain.

Above: **A cricket game is in full swing on the lawns in front of the Christchurch Boys' School. The game, which was introduced by the British, has a strong following in New Zealand.**

A game somewhat like American baseball, cricket is played with a ball and bat. Unlike baseball, however, eleven players are on each team and two goals, or wickets, are used. The pitcher, called a bowler, tries to throw the ball into the goal, which is defended by a batsman.

Introduced by the British, cricket is the oldest organized sport in New Zealand. The country has a men's national team and a women's national team, both of which play against teams from other cricket-playing countries, such as South Africa, India, Australia, and the West Indies. Within New Zealand, provincial teams compete for the Shell Cup, one of the most prestigious local honors. Cricket is also a popular sport with schoolchildren, and teams in secondary schools are particularly encouraged.

By far the most well-loved spectator sport is rugby union football, also a British game. New Zealanders are almost obsessed with rugby matches in winter. The national team, the All Blacks, has established an international reputation and is among the world's top rugby teams. It competes in the World Cup, rugby's highest level of competition, as well as in other tournaments.

Opposite: **Climbers in the Southern Alps take a break as they survey the splendor of New Zealand's mountains.**

Sailboat Racing

The America's Cup is the most sought-after prize in sailboat racing, with competitions held approximately every three to five years. In 1995, New Zealand's team, the Royal New Zealand Yacht Squadron, won the cup for the first time, beating the United States team. New Zealand retained the cup in the next contest, held in Auckland in February and March 2000, trouncing Italy's Prada team. Auckland's Annual Yachting Regatta, another major competition, is the largest one-day yachting event in the world and takes place in the waters of the city's Waitemata Harbour.

The Maori also still race war canoes. One of their races, an annual river regatta, draws people from around the country and around the world. The regatta is held on the Waikato River at Ngaruawahia, a town near Hamilton, North Island. Teams compete in rowing competitions in elaborately decorated canoes. During this event, the Maori also compete in other traditional skills, such as poi-twirling dances.

Above: **Sailboat-racing fever rises during the America's Cup and the Auckland Yachting Regatta competitions.**

EXCITEMENT IN PARIS

Bungee jumping was made famous by New Zealander A. J. Hackett when he dove off the Eiffel Tower in Paris in 1986, attached to a giant rubber bungee cord. Bungee-jumpers fall long distances off bridges, cranes, and cliffs with an adrenaline rush that lasts for days afterward.

Festivals

New Zealanders celebrate New Year's Day, Waitangi Day, Good Friday, Easter Monday, ANZAC Day, the Queen's Birthday, Labour Day, Christmas Day, and Boxing Day. A number of provinces and cities also celebrate their anniversaries. In rural areas, agricultural and pastoral (A&P) shows draw large crowds.

On February 6, New Zealanders commemorate the Treaty of Waitangi, signed in 1840 between the British and the Maori. This day is celebrated as the country's national day, although, in recent years, it has evoked mixed feelings. Many Maori see it as the day on which their culture began to decline. In 1990, for example, festivities for the 150th anniversary of the treaty were marred by large protests at the British Queen's speech.

A variety of cultural and sporting events mark Waitangi Day. Celebrations are held not only in Waitangi town, but throughout New Zealand. The prime minister usually attends a ceremony at the tribal house in Waitangi. In 2000, however, the head of government visited another marae for the first time. Disputes among the Maori, including disagreements over a woman's right to speak at a marae, resulted in the prime minister attending the formal commemoration by the Ngai Tahu tribe instead.

A&P SHOWS

Agricultural and pastoral (A&P) shows are a major part of rural life in New Zealand and have been around for over one hundred years. These shows include horseback riding and sheepshearing demonstrations and competitions for the tastiest cakes and jams and for the largest, most beautiful garden vegetables. Tents are also set up for selling agricultural equipment. A&P shows are important social occasions for farmers, who, with their families, often lead isolated lives.

Below: Children enjoy a ride on a steer at an A&P show in Rotorua.

Christmas

Christmas falls during the summer school holidays in New Zealand. Many people leave town at this time, heading for beaches or campgrounds. Some families own small, informal holiday homes. People put up Christmas trees and open presents on Christmas morning. At the midday meal, celebrants pop open party crackers, small, colorful paper cylinders that give off a loud bang when pulled open. Inside are funny hats, which people wear throughout the meal, as well as tiny toys and jokes. The dinner is traditionally lamb or turkey, followed by plum pudding or trifle, a cake soaked in liqueur, then combined with custard, fruit, and jam and topped with whipped cream.

Guy Fawkes Day

The most exciting holiday during spring is Guy Fawkes Day on November 5. Guy Fawkes, an Englishman, was hanged as a traitor in the seventeenth century after he and fellow conspirators

Below: **Christmas in New Zealand comes near the beginning of summer vacation.**

plotted to blow up the English Parliament and the king. Following English traditions, children in New Zealand use old clothes and rags to make a figure called "guy," which is then burned on top of a large bonfire at night. The celebration is also a perfect opportunity for sparklers and fireworks.

Highlands Games

The Highlands Games in Hastings are the biggest annual traditional Scottish event. People get together to perform Highland dances, play bagpipes, and throw haggis. Haggis is a traditional Scottish pudding made from of the heart and liver of a sheep or calf, minced with oatmeal and fat, and then boiled in the stomach of the animal.

ANZAC Day

The Australian and New Zealand Army Corps (ANZAC) was formed during World War I. On April 25, 1915, thousands of ANZAC soldiers lost their lives in the Battle of Gallipoli on the coast of Turkey. Today, ANZAC Day, April 25, is celebrated in New Zealand with parades and ceremonies that honor soldiers who served and died in World War I and following wars.

Food

Roast Lamb and Meat Pies

With the number of sheep farms in the country, lamb is a popular dish. Roast lamb, cooked with rosemary and garlic, is usually served with mint sauce. Lamb, along with beef, is also part of another favorite dish — meat pie, which is served with mashed potatoes, peas, and thick, brown gravy. Steak and sausages are eaten at barbecues.

Numerous fruits and vegetables grow throughout the year. The *kumara* (koo-MAH-rrah) is a kind of sweet potato that the Maori introduced into the country. It remains a popular vegetable today for both Maori and non-Maori in New Zealand.

An easy take-out food is fish and chips, which is available at any local pub or take-out diner. The fish is fried in batter and then, along with french fries, wrapped in newspaper or brown paper for the customer. In a country surrounded by oceans, it is not surprising that New Zealanders eat many kinds of seafood dishes, from cod and snapper to oysters and mussels.

Below: **In addition to roast meat and seafood, New Zealanders enjoy eating a wide variety of fruits and vegetables.**

No discussion of food is complete without including dessert. A good place to go for dessert in New Zealand is a tearoom. Open from morning to afternoon, tearooms serve a wide range of treats, including sandwiches, hot pies, cakes, tarts, and cream buns. Pavlova is a well-known dessert made of meringue, whipped cream, and fresh fruit, such as strawberries and kiwifruit, with passionfruit dribbled over the top.

Above: **A Samoan woman inspects the colorful produce at an Auckland market. In the foreground are yams, a commonly grown edible root in New Zealand. Yams were initially introduced from the Polynesian islands.**

A Traditional Maori Feast

At special Maori gatherings, the meal is cooked in a traditional earth-oven called a *hangi* (HAH-nyee). A fire is built in a pit, and stones are laid over the firewood. The heated stones are sprinkled with water and covered with leaves, and then food is placed on them. Another layer of leaves protects the food before a final layer of soil is added. The steam generated by the stones slowly cooks the food.

Lamb and pork dishes are often prepared in a hangi. It takes about three hours for meat to cook. Kumara and muttonbirds, a particular Maori delicacy, are usually part of the meal as well.

A CLOSER LOOK AT NEW ZEALAND

New Zealand's spectacular natural attractions draw visitors from all over the world. The volcanic activity that helped shape the country's islands is still evident on the North Island, where geysers shoot boiling water into the air. New Zealand's geographical isolation has resulted in unusual wildlife, including the well-known flightless birds the kiwi and kakapo.

The rugged and beautiful outdoors is the perfect setting for activities such as hiking and sailing. New Zealand's sailing team won the America's Cup, a prestigious yacht-racing competition, two consecutive times, in 1995 and 2000.

Opposite: **New Zealanders enjoy outdoor activities. Thousands take part in the Christchurch City-to-Surf Fun Run.**

New Zealanders love both watching and participating in sports. Rugby is the top spectator sport, and players on the national team, the All Blacks, are well-known celebrities.

New Zealanders have overcome their differences to forge a harmonious society. Today, people of Maori, European, and Asian descent call New Zealand home. Supported by the government, the Maori are reviving their cultural traditions. Through courage and determination, the women of New Zealand have also made a name for themselves. Famous Kiwi women include nineteenth century-suffragette Kate Sheppard, the current prime minister of the country Helen Clark, and opera star Dame Kiri Te Kanawa.

Above: **Motorists near Mosgiel, South Island, have to wait while a flock of sheep makes its way across a road.**

43

The All Blacks

"*Ka mate* (kah MAH-teh), *ka mate*, *ka ora* (kah OH-rrah), *ka ora*," chant the All Blacks rugby players, as they wildly stamp around on the field before starting a match. Every contest by the team begins with this haka, or traditional Maori war chant and dance, and this never fails to impress spectators.

The All Blacks is New Zealand's rugby union football team, and its players have become national heroes. No sport brings out more passion among New Zealanders than rugby. Rugby came to the country from Britain in the nineteenth century. Tradition has it that the game of rugby started in during a game of soccer at Rugby School in Warwickshire county, England, in 1823, when a player illegally picked up the ball.

Charles John Monro, a New Zealander sent to study in Britain, brought rugby to the town of Nelson, South Island, where he encouraged the local soccer team to try playing by rugby's rules. By 1875, the game had become established all over the colony.

Below: In a thrilling moment, a member of the All Blacks, New Zealand's national rugby union football team, receives a crucial pass and moves past his opponents.

Matches were played between provinces as well as against Australian and British teams. The New Zealand Rugby Football Union (NZRFU) was formed in 1892 to administer the game on a national basis.

Rules of the Game

In a rugby game, fifteen players are on each side — eight forwards and seven backs. Forwards are usually burly, while backs, who are relied on for their speed, have slender builds. Goal lines are 328 feet (100 m) apart. Getting the ball across the opponents' goal line and grounded is called a "try" and is worth five points. Kicking the ball through the opponents' goalposts is called a "conversion" and is worth two points.

The All Blacks team demands that its members play only for New Zealand and not accept overseas contracts. Jonah Lomu, for instance, is one of the team's most outstanding players. Because he honors his commitment to the All Blacks, Lomu has turned down high-paying contracts with overseas teams.

VICTORIES AND DEFEATS

The Rugby World Cup is now the highest level of international competition in the sport. New Zealand's All Blacks team won the very first World Cup held in 1987.
In the 1999 tournament, however, New Zealand came in fourth. Disappointment in New Zealand was intense when the All Blacks lost 31-43 to France in the semifinals. Australia ultimately won the cup.

The America's Cup

Incredible Year for New Zealand

Every few years, the America's Cup brings countries from across the globe together for a yachting competition. The trophy is the most valued prize in yachting, or sailboat racing, and the oldest trophy in international sports. New Zealand's sailors are among the top competitors. The year 2000 was an incredible year not just for fans of sailing but for almost all New Zealanders, when New Zealand won the Cup for the second time in a row.

History of the Silver Pitcher

The America's Cup competition began in 1851, when an American boat, the *America*, beat fourteen British yachts in a race in British waters. The trophy, a silver pitcher, was entrusted to the New York Yacht Club. Britain challenged the U.S. yachting club time after time, but the United States continued to win.

Other countries, such as Italy and Australia, entered the competition alongside Britain, and, in 1983, Australia won the America's Cup. The cup was soon back in the United States, however, with the San Diego Yacht Club. In 1995, the Royal New Zealand Yacht Squadron challenged the San Diego team and triumphed with its boat, *Black Magic*.

Below: **The waters of Waitemata Harbour in Auckland play host to a flotilla of colorful yachts during the Annual Auckland Yacht Regatta.**

In the year 2000, Team New Zealand geared up to defend its trophy. Italy's boat *Luna Rossa* won the semifinals, beating San Francisco's *AmericaOne*, and entered the finals against New Zealand. Both teams competed in a series of races to win the best of nine. Italy's team, Prada, never stood a chance. Team New Zealand, skippered by Russell Coutts, got off to a head start and won the first five races. Winning was as much a matter of clever boat design as good seamanship. The New Zealand boat's designers were Clay Oliver and Laurie Davidson.

Above: **National joy knew no bounds in March 2000, when New Zealand won the America's Cup for the second time in a row.**

City of Sails

Auckland was host to the 2000 America's Cup. The city is surrounded by water, with the South Pacific Ocean to the east and Tasman Sea to the west. Sailing is immensely popular here, and Auckland has been nicknamed the "City of Sails." Huge crowds watched the America's Cup races in Auckland and participated in the victory parade through the city, with Team New Zealand carrying the cup high. There were also lots of spirited cheers for the losing Italian team.

From Tea to Votes

Women's right to vote is taken for granted these days. After all, why shouldn't women vote, if men do? The answer, however, has not always been obvious. For a long time, in New Zealand, as in other countries, only men could vote. New Zealand became the first country, however, to grant women the right to vote.

Kate Sheppard was the woman behind much of the campaign for women's voting rights. Born in Liverpool, England, Kate emigrated with her mother and sister to Christchurch, New Zealand, in 1869, at the age of twenty. She became heavily involved with the Women's Christian Temperance Union (WCTU), a New Zealand society formed in 1885 to discourage drinking alcohol. At the time, heavy drinking by men was a serious problem, and a lot of public support existed for societies such as the WCTU. To provide men with an alternative to bars at lunchtime, the WCTU, taking its inspiration from similar efforts in the United States, opened tea and coffee shops.

Left: **Helen Clark, the current prime minister of New Zealand and leader of the Labour Party, casts her vote in national elections in 1996.**

Left: Queen Victoria, the British monarch who reigned between 1837 and 1901, was cited as an example of a strong woman leader by members of the Women's Christian Temperance Union in their campaign to win women the right to vote.

Within a few years of its formation, the WCTU had also begun to campaign for women's voting rights. At the time, only men participated in politics. WCTU opponents argued that a woman's place was in the home and that men would lose their respect for women if women were involved in politics. Sheppard countered these arguments by pointing out that it was unfair for women to pay taxes if they did not have a say in how taxes were spent. Women, she added, were as capable as men. She used Queen Victoria, the ruler of Britain and the colony of New Zealand at the time, as an example of a strong woman leader.

Sheppard organized meetings, wrote articles for newspapers, and collected signatures for petitions to the government. The final petition had more than 30,000 women's signatures, representing a third of the adult female population in New Zealand at that time. The document was unrolled across the length of the floor in the parliament building. Finally, on September 19, 1893, the governer signed the Electoral Bill, granting women the right to vote. Today, a woman, Helen Clark, is New Zealand's prime minister, and many women serve as politicians.

Hissing Geysers and Smoking Craters

New Zealand's spectacular landscape was shaped by volcanic activity, and some parts of the country continue to be transformed today. The largest lake in New Zealand, Lake Taupo, was created when a violent volcanic eruption left a huge crater about two thousand years ago. The surrounding region in central North Island today is still an area of high volcanic activity. Three of the area's volcanoes, Ruapehu, Tongariro, and Ngauruhoe, have continued to erupt over the last several hundred years. Mount Tarawera's eruption in 1886 and Ruapehu's in 1953 led to major disasters, each killing more than 150 people. White Island, so named by Captain Cook because it always appeared to be in a cloud of white steam, continues to erupt regularly.

Below: **The Pohutu geyser at Whakarewarewa erupts fifteen to twenty times a day and shoots about 100 feet (30 m) into the air.**

Looking for Cures

Rotorua and its surrounding areas have been popular among tourists since the 1800s. People come to marvel at the natural wonders as well as to use the waters of the area's hot springs, believed to be therapeutic. Many bath houses and hotels have spa pools fed by natural hot springs. The waters, high in mineral content, are supposed to help cure arthritis, eczema, and nervous diseases, as well as aid in recovery from illnesses. Sulfurous waters are also taken home in bottles since they are believed to be effective in treating infected cuts and bites. Some people, however, come to the baths just to relax in the hot water.

Electricity, Too

Earth's natural underground heat can be used to generate power. Drilling into the ground, engineers tap this natural energy using turbines. Powered by a moving flow of steam or gas, these engines then produce electricity. This power is known as geothermal energy. New Zealand first tapped this resource in the 1950s, around Wairakei, and the country has since continued to expand its use of geothermal energy.

Above: Geothermal power is one of New Zealand's important sources of energy. Geothermal steam found underground fuels this power station in Wairakei, North Island.

HYDROTHERMAL ACTIVITY

High underground heat flows and an abundant supply of water in the area around Rotorua have resulted in a lot of hydrothermal activity. Geysers, hot mud pools, hot springs, steaming waterfalls, and the smell of sulfur have given rise to forbidding place names, such as "Hell's Gate" or "Inferno Crater."

Keas, Kakas, and Kakapos

Mischievous or Maddening?

Why would a bird hang from a branch upside down, with one foot? Or roll over on its back, feet waving in the air, its belly exposed to another bird that is taking a flying leap? Probably because it is one of a group of keas at play. Keas are a New Zealand species of parrot and among the most mischievous and inquisitive birds in the world. They live in the Southern Alps of the South Island. The birds delight in playing for hours with each other or even by themselves, rolling stones down a hill or tossing rocks into water.

People are less than amused by their antics, however. Keas are known to wreck tents, rip open backpacks, and steal anything resembling food. Signs in parking lots in national parks now warn hikers and campers to keep an eye out for keas. Two other parrot species unique to New Zealand are the kaka and the kakapo. Both are related to the kea but are far less aggressive.

FLIGHTLESS BIRDS

New Zealand has many flightless and weak-winged birds. Moas, very large flightless birds, were hunted to extinction by the Maori. Other birds, such as penguins, takahes, kakapos, and kiwis, have been killed by animals that were introduced by the early European settlers.

Below: Keas, friendly but destructive birds, peck a car in Fiordland National Park.

An Odd Parrot

Kakapos are flightless and move around only at night. The birds are hard to spot, but courting males can be heard during the night. The males dig shallow depressions into the ground and emit deep booming sounds that can be heard for miles. They may boom all night long for several months in their attempts to attract a female. This is not an easy job, for not only are there very few females left, but the females have a hard time locating booming males. Females are also interested in mating only about every two years.

A kakapo's life is made even harder by the fact that it freezes in the face of danger. This is the worst possible defense against nonnative predators such as cats, stoats, and weasels, which are quick to kill a defenseless bird. These predators, introduced by the early European settlers, spread through New Zealand and killed off many kakapos. Now, fewer than fifty birds are left. All of these birds are on Codfish Island, a single small island that is free of predators. This island is closely monitored by New Zealand's Department of Conservation, and strict rules to protect the birds are enforced for boats and visitors arriving at the island.

ELUSIVE KAKAPOS

These nocturnal birds are so hard to find that special kakapo trackers go out with trained kakapo-tracking dogs, which sniff out the birds. Kakapos found in unprotected areas are flown by helicopter to Codfish Island. These flightless birds get to fly after all!

Kiri Te Kanawa

At the dawn of the new millennium, Kiri Te Kanawa stood poised on a small stage on the beach in Gisborne, New Zealand. Her soaring voice greeted the first few minutes of the sunrise and ushered in the year 2000. Kiri Te Kanawa, New Zealand's most renowned singer and a world-famous opera star, thus fulfilled her desire to return to her hometown for the millennium.

Opposite and *above:* **Kiri Te Kanawa, New Zealand's most renowned opera star, continues to enthrall audiences around the world.**

A Young Talent

Kiri grew up in a household that loved to sing. Her talent for singing showed at a very young age, and, by the age of six, she had been on the local radio talent show in Gisborne. Her mother, Nell, was determined to encourage this gift, and the family eventually moved to Auckland so Kiri could study with one of New Zealand's best singing teachers, Sister Mary Leo, at Saint Mary's College. Her talent developed rapidly, and she started to enter singing competitions. Her first major success was winning the Auckland Competition at the age of sixteen. Kiri's lovely voice soon made her a star throughout New Zealand.

The best place for a singer of Kiri's talent to be trained, however, was not in New Zealand but overseas, and Kiri finally went to study at the London Opera Centre in England. In an unfamiliar place and among strangers, it was difficult at first for the new student, but Kiri persevered. Her first major leading role, in 1971, was in Mozart's opera *The Marriage of Figaro*, and with it she shot straight to stardom. Her international reputation became established when she sang a few years later at the Metropolitan Opera in New York City. In 1981, she was invited to sing at the wedding of Prince Charles and Lady Diana in London, an event watched by millions on television.

What Does It Take to Be a Star?

As a teenager, Kiri Te Kanawa already had great audience appeal and a charming personality on stage. Evenings spent singing at nightclubs to earn some money added to her confidence. Her abilities to respond to the audience and to radiate her enthusiasm and joy of singing contribute greatly to her success today. Kiri celebrated her Maori roots in her recently released album, *Maori Songs* (1999), which is a collection of traditional Maori songs.

Kiwifruit

New Zealand's most famous fruit, kiwifruit, has its origins in China. Native to the Yangtze River valley in China, the fruit was first known as Chinese gooseberry. A New Zealander brought back some seeds after visiting her missionary sister in China. She passed them along, and soon, gardeners on the North Island were developing their own varieties.

The fruit was first grown as an ornamental plant in gardens, but the fruit's potential was quickly recognized by local gardeners. As the vine started to be cultivated commercially, its fruit was renamed kiwifruit after New Zealand's native bird, the kiwi. Kiwifruit's success as a crop grew rapidly in the 1970s, when the first commercial orchards were started. Its value as an export crop shot up as people around the world discovered the fruit. For many chefs, kiwifruit was a must-have. New Zealand was the only country growing it commercially at first. The fruit was marketed so successfully and prices were so good that in the 1980s, there was a rush to plant it around the country. New land was cultivated, and many citrus orchards in the Bay of Plenty region were converted to kiwifruit orchards.

WORLD CENTER FOR RESEARCH

New Zealand is the world center for research on kiwifruit. Scientists study diseases and pests of the fruit and work to develop new strains of kiwifruit. Some scientists, for example, have worked on breeding kiwifruit that would be red, instead of green, inside.

Below: **Kiwifruit is grown supported on trellises. It is a striking bright green on the inside, with many hundreds of small black seeds. The fruit is an excellent source of vitamin C.**

56

Growing Kiwifruit

Kiwifruit grows on a vine. Farmers train it along wooden or wire trellises and fences that support the vines and also make the fruit easier to harvest as pickers move between rows. The vine is grown in a sunny location, where it has some protection from the wind. Most farms are relatively small, about 10 acres (4 hectares) in size. Farmers often plant windbreaks of tall, narrow trees to protect their orchards. Since it takes five or six years after planting before a vine produces much fruit, and trellises are expensive to set up, kiwifruit can be a costly crop for farmers to start.

The first commercial kiwifruit orchards were in the Bay of Plenty region on the North Island. This area has a temperate climate and rich volcanic soils. Kiwifruit has since been planted in other parts of New Zealand as well.

Other countries have also started to grow kiwifruit. California in the United States is the primary grower outside of New Zealand. Italy, South Africa, and Chile, which have similar climates, also grow kiwifruit. New Zealand, however, is still the world's leading producer of kiwifruit.

Maori Performing Arts

From Hand Flutters to Fierce War Chants

The Maori have a rich performing arts tradition. Every hand movement in a dance means something, and the action alone tells a story. Haka, for instance, are war chants and dances that traditionally were performed just before a battle. They involve loud shouts and thunderous stamping of feet. Bulging eyes and protruding tongues make the dancers look fierce and are meant to scare the enemy.

Other dances, such as dancing with poi, a kind of ball on a string, are graceful. Women twirl the poi on long strings and flutter their hands while moving in gentle steps and singing. Dances are usually accompanied by a cappella singing and chanting. Sometimes, however, they are accompanied by a guitarist.

Left: **A Maori woman from Whakarewarewa goes through the graceful motions of a traditional dance, which involves twirling the poi, a ball on a string.**

A National Performing Arts Festival

Over two thousand Maori performers congregate every February for the Aotearoa Traditional Maori Performing Arts Festival. Most participants are part of performing groups known as kapa haka and are skilled in traditional arts, such as poi dances, haka, and various forms of singing.

Groups practice their skills throughout the year and must first compete in regional pre-qualifying rounds before they can enter this three-day national event. At the festival, groups compete for trophies in individual heats, as well as for places among the top six groups at the festival. Performances at the festival include traditional as well as original, modern compositions. To be in the top six, kapa haka have to perform in six categories. Events include a combination of dance and song categories. Finalists from the first two days of the competition compete against one another on the last day, usually a Sunday. Kapa haka that have had the most consistent quality in all events are judged the winners.

Winning kapa haka have frequently participated in the South Pacific Arts Festival, performed in opening ceremonies in the Olympics and the Commonwealth Games, taken part in Maori exhibitions in the United States, and even joined opera singer Kiri Te Kanawa in London.

Above: **Maori men in Waitangi shout and stamp as they perform a traditional war dance.**

Below: **A tattooed Maori dancer in Russell hopes his bulging eyes and protruding tongue will scare off the enemy.**

Maori Tattoos

At a traditional Maori ceremony, people gather in the large courtyard of their tribal meeting house. After a huge feast, men and women dance and share stories. Men often act out war stories, lunging at one another, clubs in hand, and tongues stuck out in defiance. Women may sing and dance, twirling and swinging poi, balls made of fiber.

On these occasions, the Maori dress in their traditional clothing of fringed flax skirts and cloaks. Both men and women may also have remarkable designs painted on their faces. Spirals, curves, and twists may cover almost the entire face of a man, while women usually have patterns on their lips and chins. These facial designs are representations of the traditional Maori art of face tattooing, or *moko* (MOH-koh). Traditional Maori moko used to be permanently tattooed on a person's face. Men could also

Below: **This Maori man, with his face painted, lunges at the enemy with his club as he acts out a war story in Waitangi.**

Left: A pattern of spirals and curves has been painted on the lips and chin of this woman from the Bay of Plenty region.

have moko on their buttocks, while women had them on their faces and chests. Moko were highly individual. They represented a person's rank in the community, and the patterns depicted details of a person's family and his or her skills and achievements.

Each formal level of ranking had its own tattoo design. A high-ranking chief, for example, could be recognized by his moko. A servant woman could similarly be identified because her nose would have a tattoo.

Getting a Tattoo

The artist who applied the moko was known as a *tohunga ta moko* (toh-HAH-nyah tah MOH-koh). He was not simply a craftsman but often a priest as well. Chanting and praying as he worked, the tohunga pricked the designs into the skin using a sharp instrument made of bone. Periodically, he rubbed black or dark greenish-black pigment, made of soot and oil or fat, into the skin. This process was extremely painful and could be done only for short periods of time. Some moko took years to complete.

TATTOOS NOW PAINTED

The importance of facial tattoos lessened after the coming of the Europeans. Many Europeans considered it barbaric, did not understand the symbolism, and gave little or no respect to Maori with tattoos showing their high rank. Today, Maori are again using the moko at ceremonies, but the tattoo is now painted on skin rather than etched permanently.

Precious Pounamu

Greenstone, or pounamu, was a prized stone among the Maori and believed to be a gift from the gods. Pounamu, which literally means "green-colored stone," is the Maori name for jades and nephrites. Valued for both its beauty and hardness, greenstone was an important material in woodworking tools such as chisels and adzes. These were used to build houses and canoes and to make elaborate wood carvings. *Mere* (MEH-reh), a flat war club and the Maori's primary weapon, was also made out of greenstone. It was a warrior's most valuable possession.

Greenstone jewelry included earrings and pendants, often in the shape of fishhooks. The most spiritually significant were the *tiki* (tee-KEE), worn in remembrance of one's ancestors.

Better Than Gold?

Greenstone is found only on the western coast of the South Island. Gathering it involved long and difficult expeditions by

Above: **The Maori used greenstone to make earrings and pendants, often in the shape of fishhooks.**

Left: **Small greenstone figures known as tiki are worn as pendants. Tiki usually depict warriors with their tongue stuck out in defiance and are believed to have great spiritual power.**

the Maori across the mountains of the Southern Alps. Small search parties from the eastern part of the island left on journeys that could take several months. They blazed new trails across the rugged mountains, crossed swollen rivers, and searched for mountain passes.

Also a spiritual task, the gathering of greenstone required appropriate timing and rituals. The leader of a search party went through religious ceremonies and asked for guidance from the spirits. When a new boulder of greenstone was found, it was named after the spirit that had helped the searchers.

By the 1500s, greenstone was an important part of trade across both North and South Islands and became the principal medium of exchange. Power in some areas was built primarily around greenstone supplies. Once iron was introduced by the Europeans, however, the Maori switched to iron tools, and the use of pounamu declined. The beautiful stone is still used today to make jewelry and other ornaments.

Above: **The trails in Fiordland National Park that were established by the Maori and the passes they discovered are still in use today. Many popular walking tracks, such as the Heaphy Track, Harper Pass, and Routeburn Track, are former greenstone trails.**

Saving Lake Manapouri

New Zealanders are very protective of the great beauty of their country's landscape. New Zealand has many plants and animals not found anywhere else in the world. The Department of Conservation is a government body charged with preserving the natural heritage of the country. Other organizations, such as Greenpeace and the Royal Forest and Bird Protection Society, also play important roles. Children can participate through the Kiwi Conservation Club.

Electricity or the Environment?

The campaign to save Lake Manapouri in the 1970s was the first time a large part of the population rallied around the protection of a natural area. At stake were two lakes in Fiordland National Park — Lake Manapouri and Lake Te Anau. Water from both is used by a power plant that generates electricity. Power output depends on the height of a lake above sea level and how much water can be directed to flow continuously.

Below: **Surrounded by mountains, beautiful beech forests, and beaches, Lake Manapouri is considered one of the loveliest lakes in New Zealand.**

Engineers wanted to raise the level of the lake artificially to generate more energy and, thereby, have a steady supply of electricity for an aluminum producing plant, Comalco. The government planned to give the go-ahead, but a group of citizens became concerned that the swampy and low-lying fertile areas around the lake would be flooded, destroying rare plant life.

Above: **New Zealanders take great care to preserve the untouched environment of their wilderness areas, such as the area around the Church of the Good Shepherd on the shores of Lake Tekapo, South Island.**

Save Manapouri

Ronald McLean, a local farmer, was the driving force behind the Save Manapouri Campaign. He and his daughter went on a road tour in the summer of 1969. They presented slides at meetings and talked to people. Television programs and newspapers cried out for alternatives to interfering with the lake. Before long, Save Manapouri branches mushroomed around the land, and letters were pouring into the McLean home. The tourism and recreation industries banded together with conservationists to save the lake. By 1970, the largest petition in the history of the country had been delivered to the parliament. The government decided to postpone a decision on lake levels, although it was not until 1981 that the lakes received legal protection.

Sheep

For much of New Zealand's history since European settlement, sheep were the backbone of the country's economy. Sheep still play a major role today, with New Zealand being one of the largest exporters of wool, lamb, and mutton in the world.

Early European settlers in the nineteenth century cleared forests and burned grasslands to create pasture. They brought in a breed of sheep known as merinos from Australia, and these became the basis for sheep farming in the country.

A different breed, the Romney sheep, was introduced later, and Romneys are now preferred for both their lambs and their strong, coarse wool. Wool from Romneys is used for making

Below: **Sheep near Rotorua are sorted into holding pens before they are sheared.**

carpets and rugs. Some farms specialize in sheep with brown or black wool and raise only these varieties.

The mild climate allows sheep to be grazed year-round in most of the country. Most of New Zealand's sheep farms are small family farms, although a few sheep stations cover very large areas. Some farms are so isolated that the sheep farmers' children have to go to boarding school. In the mountainous countryside, shepherds rely on dogs and motorbikes to manage and patrol the flocks.

How Many Sheep Can You Shear?

Spring is the time to shear sheep for their wool. Sheepshearers travel from farm to farm during the season. They often stay on the farm in shearing quarters, shearing between 250 and 300 sheep in one day.

Sheepshearers can show off their skills at sheepshearing competitions. Many such competitions are held around New Zealand. The largest is the Golden Shears Championship, which takes place every March.

This competition began in the 1960s and was so popular in its early years that spectators had to book seats twelve months in advance. New Zealand sheepshearers were soon ready to challenge their neighboring Australian counterparts, and in 1980 the first World Shearers Championships were held.

Below: **Shearers show off their skills in the sheepshearing contest at the Mayfield Show in the Canterbury region, South Island.**

Sheepshearers compete on speed, precision, and the quality of their shearing. David Fagan of Te Kuiti, North Island, is a champion shearer. In the March 2000 competition of the Golden Shears Championship, he had the fastest shearing time and won the Golden Shears Open title for the twelfth time.

Others compete in wool pressing or wool handling. Wool pressing is among the most demanding of physical activities. Wool pressers have to tramp and press several thousand pounds (kilograms) of wool a day.

Three Cities, Three Histories

The history of New Zealand is, in many ways, the history of its settlements. At first glance, Christchurch feels like a small English town. Dunedin, on the other hand, is uniquely Scottish in heritage, while Akaroa still retains the feel of a provincial French village.

Christchurch

Christchurch in the Canterbury region is considered the most English of New Zealand's towns. The settlement was established in 1850 when the Canterbury Association in Britain sent its first set of immigrants to New Zealand. The nearby Canterbury Plains had some of the best farming land, and, as sheep farming flourished, Christchurch became the central market town for the Canterbury Plains. A river called the Avon runs through Christchurch and is named after the Avon River in Britain.

Below: **A punt floats down the Avon River, which winds through Christchurch, South Island.**

Dunedin

Dunedin is the Gaelic name for Edinburgh, the capital of Scotland. The New Zealand settlement of Dunedin was founded in the nineteenth century by Scottish immigrants. Led by Captain William Walter Cargill, the first Scottish settlers arrived in 1848 on board the ship *John Wickliffe*. The *Philip Laing* followed a few months later. By the end of that year, the new town of Dunedin had been established.

Akaroa

Akaroa is a town on French Bay in the Canterbury region. As the bay's name might indicate, Akaroa was established by French settlers and was actually the first French settlement in New Zealand. A French whaler, Jean Langlois, negotiated the purchase of the land from the Maori in 1838. He returned to France to form a trading company, the Nanto-Bordelaise Company. Langlois came back to Akaroa in August 1840. This time he was accompanied by about eighty French colonists.

FRENCH HERITAGE IN AKAROA

Akaroa's early French settlers planted some of the original grapevines that started the wine industry in the Canterbury region. A number of street names in Akaroa are French, including rue Lavaud, rue Balguerie, and rue Jolie. *Rue* means "street" in the French language.

Tramping

People hiking or trekking in New Zealand are said to be "tramping." They tramp not on trails, but on tracks, routes, or walks. Walks are the easiest, while routes are the most rugged and the least well-marked. Both visitors and New Zealanders love to explore the country's spectacular landscape, particularly during the summer months, from November through April. The main areas for tramping are in the national parks and along the Southern Alps. Tracks, which usually take three to five days to traverse, pass through a range of scenery, from mountains to river valleys, lakes, and beaches. Most tracks have huts along them, which provide a place to sleep and a stove on which to cook.

The Great Walks

The Great Walks are the most popular walks. These include the Heaphy Track, Milford Track, Rakiura Track, and Routeburn Track. Since they are so popular, they require special passes. Milford Track, located in Fiordland National Park, is known

Below: **The Kepler Track in Fiordland National Park is a favorite with trekkers. The track usually takes about four days to complete.**

around the world. It follows a river valley, passes up through rain forests over the Mackinnon Pass, past Sutherland Falls, the country's highest waterfall, and down to Milford Sound. Although catching a fine day in this region is next to impossible, since Milford may get more than 240 inches (610 cm) of rain a year, trampers are rarely deterred from traversing the Milford Track.

Above: **Trampers in Fiordland National Park take a break. A tent is essential as the area receives heavy rains.**

Staying Alert

The landscape may indeed be beautiful, but trampers need to be aware of the dangers as well. The greatest dangers are encountered when crossing rivers and when temperatures fall suddenly. Rivers rise and fall quickly during storms. Only the main tracks have bridges, so trampers may have to wait a day or so to cross rivers after a sudden flood. The changeable weather also leads to the risk of hypothermia, or sudden chilling, which can cause illness and confusion. Areas high up in the mountains sometimes have sudden snowstorms, even in the middle of summer. Experienced trampers therefore avoid cotton clothing (which stays wet) and wear wool or synthetic materials.

Treaty of Waitangi

The Treaty of Waitangi is commemorated every year on Waitangi Day, February 6. Although broadly celebrated as symbolizing the birth of New Zealand as a nation, Waitangi Day has also become a day of protests for the Maori. The Treaty of Waitangi was originally drawn up by the British government in 1840. The treaty was intended to lessen friction between the Maori and the European settlers. It gave new settlers the right to stay in New Zealand, while also guaranteeing the Maori rights to their lands, forests, and fisheries in exchange for their acknowledgment of British rule. Over fifty Maori chiefs signed the treaty.

The treaty did not solve the problems surrounding land ownership, however. Pressure for land by the new settlers grew. The treaty was ignored, and much Maori land was taken by the settlers by force or through trickery. The treaty was never ratified by the New Zealand parliament, and it essentially died. In the 1960s, however, Maori culture underwent a revival, and the Maori

Below: **Maori chiefs and William Hobson, who represented the British Crown, signed the Treaty of Waitangi at Treaty House in Waitangi on February 6, 1840.**

began making claims for compensation for land taken away from them. Maori took to the streets, formed power groups, and occupied pieces of land. The Treaty of Waitangi started to play a dominant role in their demands.

Maori Stake Their Claims

The government finally introduced the Waitangi Tribunal in 1975 to hear complaints and investigate land claims by the Maori. Maori individuals or groups can make claims before the tribunal if they feel the government has allowed something to happen that goes against the promises of the treaty. Claims range from large to small. For instance, in one of the largest recent claims, five Maori tribes have asked for compensation for lands taken from them in central North Island, and for the return of seven forests and many lakes and rivers, including fourteen lakes around Rotorua.

Claims can take many years to be settled. In 1995, the Tainui tribe received NZ $170 million for lands confiscated from their ancestors in 1884. The New Zealand government hopes that all claims can be settled by the year 2010 and that the Waitangi Tribunal can then be disbanded.

Above: **The Treaty House in Waitangi was built in 1832 as the home of the British Resident. Eight years later, the Treaty of Waitangi was signed there. Today, it is preserved as a memorial and museum, and is a popular tourist attraction in the Northland region of the North Island.**

RELATIONS WITH NORTH AMERICA

New Zealand, the United States, and Canada share a common history as former British colonies. New Zealand is a much younger country, however, and it did not become a British colony until the mid-nineteenth century. The country's great distance from the United States and Canada meant that early connections were limited.

During its early years as a colony, New Zealand primarily attracted American whalers in search of whale oil and sealskin. Russell, on the North Island, was an important stopping place for

Opposite: **A team from New Zealand competed at the Winter Olympics in Nagano, Japan, in 1998. New Zealand is also expected to compete at the 2002 Winter Olympic Games in Salt Lake City, Utah.**

food and water, and whalers traded with the Maori, giving Maori muskets and rum. In the 1850s, gold discoveries first drew New Zealanders to California and later, Californians to New Zealand.

Today, relations between New Zealand, the United States, and Canada are much more developed. Trade has increased, and New Zealand is working to expand its export market in North America. New Zealand and the United States have also worked closely together on several environmental issues and have had particular success on efforts to protect Antarctica.

Above: **A forestry worker cuts timber in the forests of Tapanui in the Southland region of the South Island. The processing of forest products for the American market forms an important sector of the New Zealand economy.**

The Lure of Gold

The word *gold* echoed around the Pacific Rim in the mid-nineteenth century, starting with the discovery of gold on the banks of the Sacramento River in California in January 1848. Word reached New Zealand by the end of that year, with reports appearing in the newspaper *The New Zealander*. Thousands of people from both New Zealand and Australia sailed to California to try their luck at finding gold. Australian ships stopped over in New Zealand for food or repairs and, in the process, often picked up new passengers. New Zealanders outfitted their own vessels as well, with Auckland becoming the primary hub for ships sailing to California. Once in California, however, life was hard. Finding gold was not that easy, living costs were extremely high, and jobs were hard to find.

The tide of immigration was reversed in the 1850s, when gold was discovered in both Australia and New Zealand. In 1861, the New Zealand gold rush began with the discovery of large quantities of gold in the Otago region, South Island. Gabriel Read, a Tasmanian who had also tried his luck in the California goldfields, found gold near Tuapeka River. This site was named Gabriel's Gully. He was quick to share the news, and once word spread, thousands of miners from the goldfields of California and Australia flocked to New Zealand.

Below: **Arrow River and Shotover River in the Otago region of the South Island attracted many thousands of prospectors when gold was discovered there in the 1860s.**

Immigration

Americans quickly fall in love with New Zealand's beautiful landscape and its friendly people. Many go as tourists, but some also go there to work, especially in the technical fields. New Zealand encourages Americans to visit and to work and allows them to buy property there.

Some New Zealanders move to the United States or Canada, often to study or search for jobs. Some stay on for many years, others for the rest of their lives. Some of the larger cities, including San Francisco, New York, Houston, Phoenix, Montreal, and Toronto, have New Zealand clubs or associations where fellow New Zealanders can meet. They get together to celebrate national holidays such as Waitangi Day and ANZAC Day. During the rest of the year, they may get together for monthly pub nights, hikes, picnics, or potluck meals. The America's Cup races are followed with avid interest. New Zealanders' love and knowledge of the ocean is evident in their San Francisco club, which has an annual adventure sail around the bay. In Toronto and Houston, New Zealanders have formed clubs jointly with Australians.

Above: **Americans and other tourists love the quaint old-world charm of New Zealand. The tourists shown here are in line for a tram ride through the historic parts of Christchurch, South Island.**

Trade and Alliances

Relations between New Zealand and North America were limited during their early histories because of distance. That limiting factor has been overcome in recent decades. With the growth of e-commerce and Internet businesses, trade between the United States and New Zealand has increased dramatically. American investors have become increasingly interested in establishing bases in New Zealand for industries that can operate over the Internet. New Zealand's trade with the United States also grew during the Asian economic crisis of the late 1990s, and exports to the United States rose by 30 percent.

New Zealand and the United States are also military allies. During World War II, American forces provided the primary defense for New Zealand against Japan. On September 1, 1951, Australia, New Zealand, and the United States signed a collective defensive agreement called the ANZUS Treaty. Under this treaty, the three countries promised to come to one another's defense in case of attack. The continued effectiveness of the treaty, however, is doubtful following New Zealand's adoption of a strong antinuclear policy.

Above: **American troops played a key role in the defense of South Pacific territories during World War II.**

A DOUBTFUL TREATY

In 1984, the New Zealand government decided to ban from its ports all ships carrying nuclear weapons or propelled by nuclear fuel. In 1985, a U.S. destroyer was denied access. The U.S. government responded by canceling ANZUS exercises and meetings. It announced that it could no longer guarantee security under the ANZUS Treaty. New Zealand, however, continues its stand against nuclear-equipped warships.

Asia-Pacific Economic Cooperation

Despite strained military relations, the United States and New Zealand work together closely on trade issues. Both belong to the Asia-Pacific Economic Cooperation (APEC), a group of twenty-one regional economies that was formed to promote economic cooperation in the Asia-Pacific area. The United States played a key role in the formation of this group and initiated yearly meetings. In 1999, the annual meeting of APEC was held in Auckland, New Zealand. U.S. president Bill Clinton traveled to Auckland for three days of APEC meetings. While in the country, he also visited the International Antarctic Centre in Christchurch and went skiing in the Southern Alps with his daughter, Chelsea.

Left: **U.S. president Bill Clinton speaks at a press conference during his visit to Christchurch in September 1999. Jenny Shipley, New Zealand's prime minister at that time, is in the background. This visit was the first by a U.S. president in thirty-six years.**

Left: **Carol Mosely Braun (*left*), the U.S. ambassador to New Zealand, exchanges a traditional Maori greeting with Sir Henare Ngata, a Maori elder and statesman, during a celebration to welcome the new millennium.**

Ambassadors' Vital Roles

Ambassadors play important roles in maintaining relations between countries, fostering trade, and providing moral support to citizens of their own country. Jim Bolger, New Zealand's ambassador to the United States, traveled around the United States in early 2000, meeting Kiwis. He listened to their concerns about returning to their country, encouraged them to step up trade, and advised them on the buying of property.

Carol Moseley Braun, a former U.S. senator from Illinois, was appointed ambassador to New Zealand in 1999. Vice-President Al Gore presided over her swearing-in ceremony on December 9, 1999. Ambassador Moseley Braun has the distinction of having been only the second African-American in the U.S. Senate during the twentieth century and the first woman senator from Illinois.

The American Embassy in New Zealand supports Fulbright New Zealand, a cultural exchange program that allows New Zealand and American students to study and undertake research in each other's country. This program has been running for more than fifty years and has been instrumental in building people-to-people links between the United States and New Zealand.

Cultural Relations

Americans learn about New Zealand either through traveling there or through the arts exhibitions and performance troupes that visit the United States. New Zealand's role in the world of cinema has also grown recently, and the country draws Americans interested in various aspects of film production.

Over the years, some New Zealand artists have looked to American artists for inspiration. Frank Sargeson (1903–1982), whose short stories are classics in New Zealand, was greatly influenced by American writers, particularly Sherwood Anderson (1876–1941). Sargeson became the best-known short-story writer and novelist of his time and mentored an entire generation of New Zealand writers who later became famous in their own right.

Louis Hay, a modern New Zealand architect, became greatly interested in the work of the pioneering American architect Frank Lloyd Wright (1867–1959). Many of his designs show the influence of Wright's Prairie style, developed in the United States during the early twentieth century.

PRAIRIE STYLE

American architect Frank Lloyd Wright has influenced the architecture of modern homes in New Zealand. His Prairie style was developed during the early twentieth century. Prairie style houses tend to be simple, unadorned buildings, with spacious rooms that are designed for comfort and convenience.

Left: American architect Frank Lloyd Wright inspects an architectural model.

As Far South As You Can Go

For those with an interest in the cold southern continent, New Zealand is a stepping stone to Antarctica. Travelers use Christchurch as their last stop before heading for Antarctica. The Antarctic has become the focus of a major cooperative research program between the United States and New Zealand. The International Antarctic Centre in Christchurch is the headquarters for the U.S. research program, the United States Antarctic Program, and the New Zealand research program, Antarctica New Zealand. Among other projects, researchers monitor the Antarctic ozone hole. During his 1999 visit to New Zealand, U.S. president Bill Clinton visited the International Antarctic Centre and announced that New Zealand scientists and those of other nations would henceforth have access to U.S. satellite images of the Antarctic.

For those not making it as far as the Antarctic itself, visiting the International Antarctic Centre is the next best thing. The Centre tries to recreate the atmosphere of Antarctica, with snow caves, polar survival clothing, snowmobiles, videos of penguins, and opportunities to meet the actual researchers.

Below: **U.S. president Bill Clinton delivers an address during a visit to the International Antarctic Centre in Christchurch in September 1999, as famed New Zealand explorer Sir Edmund Hillary and then Prime Minister Jenny Shipley sit listening in the background.**

The International Antarctic Centre welcomes President Clinton to Christchurch, New Zealand

The America's Cup: An Exciting Tussle

The America's Cup is the most valued prize in yacht-racing, and teams from both New Zealand and the United States are avid participants. Races are held approximately every three to five years. The United States was the first to win the cup, in 1851, with its schooner *America*. The New York Yacht Club successfully defended the cup for 132 years, until 1983, when it lost to Australia's team. During that period, well-known Americans, including Cornelius Vanderbilt and William Rockefeller, competed in these races.

In 1995, New Zealand won the cup for the first time when the Royal New Zealand Yacht Squadron triumphed against *Young America* from the San Diego Yacht Club. New Zealand's first victory was a cause for great national celebration. The U.S. team was led by skipper Dennis Conner, who had won the America's Cup three times.

New Zealand's team, led by skipper Russell Coutts, sailed to victory again in the 2000 competition, beating Italy. New Zealand is the only other country besides the United States to successfully defend the Cup.

Above: **In March 2000, New Zealand successfully defended the America's Cup, which it won for the first time in 1995.**

The Movie World

New Zealand's movies and actors have become well known in North America over the last few decades. Film director Jane Campion rose to prominence in the United States with the release of her 1993 film *The Piano*, which won the Academy Award for Best Original Screenplay.

Enjoying similar success was Anna Paquin, also a New Zealander, who played the role of a child in that same movie. She was cast in the role at the age of nine; by the age of twelve, she had become the first New Zealander to receive an Oscar for Best Supporting Actress. Paquin, now a teenager, spends her time between film-shooting locations in Los Angeles and her home in Wellington, New Zealand.

Perhaps even more widely known is actress Lucy Lawless. She has the title role in the television series, "Xena, Warrior Princess," which is produced by Universal Studios. Lawless was born in Auckland and lived briefly in Canada, where she studied drama at the William Davis Centre for Actors in Vancouver.

Below: **Lucy Lawless talks with host Jay Leno on the set of "The Tonight Show with Jay Leno" in Burbank, California.**

Noted Actor and Filmmaker

Sam Neill, another well-known Kiwi actor, got his start participating in drama productions at his boarding school and at the University of Canterbury, both in Christchurch. He worked in Australia for many years making documentary films. He became widely known in the United States when he acted in the 1993 Steven Spielberg film *Jurassic Park*.

He has filmed a number of movies in the United States. One of them, *The Horse Whisperer*, starring Robert Redford, was filmed in Montana and New York in 1997. In 1999, he worked in San Francisco with Robin Williams on the film *Bicentennial Man*. Neill has also worked in Hawaii, playing the role of the politician Walter Murray Gibson in *Molokai* (1999), a film based on the true story of Father Damien, who cared for Hawaiian lepers in the nineteenth century, and who himself died from the disease. Neill also starred as the wizard in the miniseries "Merlin," which brought NBC a television ratings victory in April 1998. The first half of the miniseries was watched by almost 37 million viewers.

MAORI ACTORS IN HOLLYWOOD

Cliff Curtis is a Maori actor from Rotorua who has become an international movie star. He has acted in many films, including *Six Days, Seven Nights* (1998) with Harrison Ford. Cliff Curtis values his Maori culture and has rejected roles that reinforce prejudice against indigenous peoples. Temeura Morrison is a fellow Maori actor, also from Rotorua. He and Curtis both starred in *Once Were Warriors* (1995), which deals with Maori culture in a changing world.

NEW ZEALAND

Regional Boundary
■ **Capital**
● **City**
River

1

Waitangi ● Russell
1
● Whangarei

2

North
Island

N

Auckland ●
Coromandel
Peninsula
2

White Island

Ngaruawahia ● 3 ● Tauranga
Hamilton ● ● Te Puke
Waikato R.
Te Kuiti ● Rotorua ● 4 5
Whakarewarewa ● ● Mt. Tarawera
Whakapapa ● Wairakei ● Gisborne
Lake
Taupo
TASMAN SEA
7 *Mt. Tongariro*
(6,458 ft/1,968 m)
Mt. Taranaki (8,261 ft/2,518 m) ▲ Napier 6
Mt. Ngauruhoe (7,517 ft/2,291 m) ▲
Mt. Ruapehu (9,177 ft/2,797 m) ▲ ● Hastings

3

Wanganui ●
Ratana ● 8

Tasman
Bay
10
9
Nelson ● 11
Lake
Rotoroa 12 *Cook Strait*
■ WELLINGTON

13

Mt. Tasman (11,477 ft / 3,498 m)
Mt. Cook (12,349 ft / 3,764 m) ▲ *Tasman*
Glacier
Mt. Sefton ▲ 14
La Perouse ▲
● Christchurch

4

Milford Sound
Fiordland
National
Park
Arrow
River
Shotover River
Lake
Tekapo
Canterbury Plains
● Akaroa

South

SOUTH PACIFIC OCEAN

Lake
Te Anau
Lake
Wakatipu
15
Island

Lake Manapouri
16
Sutherland
Falls
Mosgiel ● ● Dunedin
● Tapanui
Gabriel's
Gully
Tuapeka River

5

● Invercargill

Codfish
Island
Stewart
Island

REGIONS

1 **NORTHLAND**
2 **AUCKLAND**
3 **WAIKATO**
4 **BAY OF PLENTY**
5 **GISBORNE**
6 **HAWKE'S BAY**
7 **TARANAKI**
8 **MANAWATU-**
WANGANUI
9 **WELLINGTON**
10 **TASMAN**
11 **NELSON**
12 **MARLBOROUGH**
13 **WEST COAST**
14 **CANTERBURY**
15 **OTAGO**
16 **SOUTHLAND**

Chatham Island

Chatham Island

Pitt Island

Above: A boy helps his father round up sheep that strayed from the main flock.

Akaroa B4
Arrow River A4
Auckland C2

Canterbury Plains B4
Chatham Island D5
Chatham Islands D5
Christchurch B4
Codfish Island A5
Cook Strait C3
Coromandel Peninsula C1-C2

Dunedin B5

Fiordland National Park A4-A5

Gabriel's Gully A5
Gisborne D2

Hamilton C2
Hastings C3

Invercargill A5

La Perouse A4

Lake Manapouri A5
Lake Rotoroa B3
Lake Taupo C2
Lake Te Anau A5
Lake Tekapo B4
Lake Wakatipu A5

Milford Sound A4
Mosgiel B5
Mt. Cook A4
Mt. Ngauruhoe C2
Mt. Ruapehu C3
Mt. Sefton A4
Mt. Taranaki C2
Mt. Tarawera C2
Mt. Tasman A4-B4
Mt. Tongariro C2

Napier C2
Nelson B3
Ngaruawahia C2
North Island B1-C3

Pitt Island D5

Ratana C3

Rotorua C2
Russell C1

Shotover River A4
South Island A5-C3
South Pacific Ocean C5-D4
Southern Alps A4-B4
Stewart Island A5
Sutherland Falls A5

Tapanui A5
Tasman Bay B3
Tasman Glacier B4
Tasman Sea A3-B2

Tauranga C2
Te Kuiti C2
Te Puke C2
Tuapeka River A5-B5

Waikato River C2
Wairakei C2
Waitangi C1
Wanganui C3
Wellington C3
Whakapapa C2
Whakarewarewa C2
Whangarei C1
White Island C2

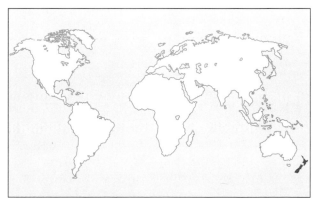

NEW ZEALAND

N

How Is Your Geography?

Learning to identify the main geographical areas and points of a country can be challenging. Although it may seem difficult at first to memorize the locations and spellings of major cities or the names of mountain ranges, rivers, deserts, lakes, and other prominent physical features, the end result of this effort can be very rewarding. Places you previously did not know existed will suddenly come to life when referred to in world news, whether in newspapers, television reports, or other books and reference sources. This knowledge will make you feel a bit closer to the rest of the world, with its fascinating variety of cultures and physical geography.

Used in a classroom setting, the instructor can make duplicates of this map using a copy machine. (PLEASE DO NOT WRITE IN THIS BOOK!) Students can then fill in any requested information on their individual map copies. Used one-on-one, the student can also make copies of the map on a copy machine and use them as a study tool. The student can practice identifying place names and geographical features on his or her own.

Above: **The beauty of the majestic Southern Alps is reflected in this mountain lake.**

New Zealand at a Glance

Official Name New Zealand

Capital Wellington

Official Languages English and Maori

Population 3.8 million

Land Area 103,737 square miles (268,680 square km)

Major Islands North Island, South Island

Highest Point Mount Cook 12,349 feet (3,764 m)

Longest River Waikato 264 miles (425 km)

Largest Lake Lake Taupo 234 square miles (606 square km)

Main Ethnic Groups New Zealand European 74.5%, Maori 9.7%, other European 4.6%, Pacific Islander 3.8%, Asian and others 7.4%

Main Religions Anglican 24%, Presbyterian 18%, Roman Catholic 15%, Methodist 5%, Baptist 2%, other Protestant 3%, unspecified or none 33%

National Anthem "God Defend New Zealand"

National Plant Pohutukawa

National Bird Kiwi

Largest City Auckland

Important Anniversary Waitangi Day (February 6)

Famous Personalities Sir Edmund Hillary — first to climb Mount Everest
Dame Kiri Te Kanawa — world-famous opera star

Exports Beef, cheese, chemicals, fish, forestry products, fruits and vegetables, lamb, mutton, wool

Imports Aircraft, consumer goods, equipment, machinery, petroleum, plastics, vehicles

Currency New Zealand dollar (NZ $2.21725 = U.S. $1 as of 2000)

Opposite: **This Maori boy attempts to look fierce as he lunges with a spear in a traditional war dance.**

Glossary

Maori Vocabulary

Aotearoa (ah-oh-tay-ah-RROH-ah): the Maori name for New Zealand, literally meaning "land of the long white cloud."

haere mai (hay-REH mah-EE): welcome.

haere ra (hay-REH rrah): farewell.

haka (HAH-kah): war dances/chants.

*hangi (*HAH-nyee): a traditional earth-oven; also the word for a Maori feast.

hapu (HAH-poo): subtribe.

iwi (ee-WEE): tribe.

ka mate (kah MAH-teh): "It is death;" part of the chant used in traditional haka.

ka ora (kah OH-rrah): "It is life;" part of the chant used in traditional haka.

kapa haka (KAH-pah HAH-kah): performing groups.

kia ora (kee-ah OH-rrah): hello.

kumara (koo-MAH-rrah): a type of sweet potato grown by the Maori.

marae (mah-rah-EE): the sacred space in front of a traditional meeting house; also sometimes refers to the ancestral village of a tribe.

mere (MEH-reh): a Maori weapon.

moko (MOH-koh): facial tattoo.

pakeha (pah-KEH-hah): the term used for New Zealanders of European descent.

poi (poh-EE): a ball woven of flax fiber.

pounamu (poo-NAH-moo): greenstone.

poupou (POO-poo): carved wooden figures decorating a marae.

te kohanga reo (teh koh-HAH-nyah RREH-oh): schools where Maori children are taught Maori language and culture.

tiki (tee-KEE): small, greenstone figures usually worn as pendants.

tohunga ta moko (toh-HAH-nyah tah MOH-koh): a Maori teacher; a learned person who also does moko.

tukutuku (too-koo-TOO-koo): decorative wall paneling, or a design that resembles it.

wai (wah-EE): water.

English Vocabulary

a cappella: singing without the accompaniment of instruments.

adrenaline: a substance produced by the body when excited, scared, or angry. It gives the body more energy and causes the heart to beat faster.

affiliation: a close or official connection with a particular group of people, such as a church or political party.

arthritis: inflammation of one or more of the joints in the body that causes much pain and swelling.

autocratic: describing one who is in complete control and who makes decisions without consulting others.

backbone: the main supporting part that gives strength to the whole unit.

campaigns: series of activities planned with a particular objective in mind.

compensation: a sum of money or property given as payment or restitution for injury or loss.

confiscated: took away; seized.

conservation: the protection, preservation, and study of animal and plant life.

conspirators: people who secretly agree among themselves to commit a crime.

constellation: a group of stars that forms an identifiable pattern in the night sky and has a name. Orion, for example, is a constellation.

cults: religious groups that are extreme or controversial in their practices.

denominations: branches of a religious organization.

discrimination: the unfair treatment of certain people based on a prejudice.

dominant: major; important.

eczema: a disease of the skin in which it itches, blisters, and becomes sore.

expedition: a journey made for a particular purpose, such as exploration.

friction: disagreement; conflict.

geysers: underground springs that occasionally shoot out fountains of hot water and steam.

glaciers: large masses of ice and snow that move very slowly down a mountain or across land.

guaranteeing: promising officially to uphold an obligation, usually in return for another act.

heritage: the qualities, traditions, and features of life that a group of people have passed down from one generation to another.

immigrants: people who move into a foreign country to make their homes.

independent: separate; self-governing.

inspiration: a source of ideas or motivation for works of art.

isolation: separation from others.

liqueur: a sweet, flavored type of alcoholic drink.

millennium: a period of 1,000 years.

muskets: guns with long barrels that were used before the invention of the rifle.

mythology: the collection of legends and fables of a particular people.

nephrites: types of jade stones.

nocturnal: active at or occurring during the night.

ornamental: having a decorative purpose.

patriotism: strong love and support of one's own country.

petitions: signed papers given to people in authority to formally request benefits or rights.

pigment: a substance used to give color to other materials.

progressive: modern; forward-looking.

prospectors: people who look for gold, oil, and other natural resources in the ground or under the sea.

ratified: formally approved.

regatta: a sailing race or an organized series of such races.

rituals: the series of words and actions that make up a religious ceremony.

seamanship: knowledge and skill related to the navigation, safety, and maintenance of a ship.

statutes: laws made and enacted by a government.

suffragette: a woman in the late nineteenth and early twentieth centuries who was involved in the campaign to give women the right to vote.

symbolism: the use of visible signs, objects, or art to give meaning and significance.

therapeutic: having a soothing, healing effect on illnesses.

More Books to Read

Deep River Talk: Collected Poems. Hone Tuwhare and Frank Stewart (translator) (University of Hawaii Press)

Fiordland Underwater: New Zealand's Hidden Wilderness. Paddy Ryan and Chris Paulin (Exisle Publishing)

Heart of Gold: The People and Places of Otago. Ian Dougherty (Exisle Publishing)

A Home by the Sea: Protecting Coastal Wildlife. Kenneth Mallory (Gulliver Books)

Kea, Bird of Paradox. Judy Diamond and Alan B. Bond (University of California Press)

Land of the Long White Cloud: Maori Myths, Tales, and Legends. Kiri Te Kanawa (Trafalgar Square)

The Moas. Katie Beck (Landmark Editions)

My Mysterious World. Margaret Mahy (Richard C. Owen Publishing)

New Zealand. Cultures of the World series. Roselynn Smelt (Benchmark)

New Zealand. Enchantment of the World series. Mary Virginia Fox (Children's Press)

New Zealand. Festivals of the World series. Jonathan Griffiths (Gareth Stevens)

Videos

Anyplace Wild: Trekking and Climbing in New Zealand. (PBS Home Video)

New Zealand. (IVN Entertainment)

New Zealand Safari. (Brentwood Communications)

Web Sites

maori.culture.co.nz

www.newzealand.com/index.html

www.doc.govt.nz/cons/native/native.htm

www.nzemb.org/backgrounder/geninfo.htm

Due to the dynamic nature of the Internet, some web sites stay current longer than others. To find additional web sites, use a reliable search engine with one or more of the following keywords to help you locate information about New Zealand. Keywords: *All Blacks, Auckland, Dunedin, kiwi, Maoris, Mount Cook, Wellington.*

Index